"This is a great treasure for anyone attempting to connect faith with life. I'd like to put this book into the hands of every person who has ever faced a personal struggle. Loretta Girzaitis is a gifted storyteller who makes the presence of God more real than ever." **Bill Huebsch,** author, teacher, and founder of the Vatican II Center

"*Raised to the Light* is a rich collection of stories that provides inspiration for all the seasons of our lives. Each one witnesses to an encounter with grace. In addition, Girzaitis's poems, which gently punctuate the end of each story, invite readers to reflect on their own experience of the Spirit in their lives and to claim the wisdom it holds. A wonderful daily companion! **Rev. Sue Campbell,** minister, United Church of Canada

RAISED
TO THE
LIGHT

RAISED

TO THE

LIGHT

Stories of Hope and Transformation

by
Loretta Girzaitis

Saint Mary's Press
Christian Brothers Publications
Winona, Minnesota

The publishing team included Carl Koch, development editor; Laurie A. Berg, copy editor; James H. Gurley, production editor; Hollace Storkel, typesetter; Stephan Nagel, art director; Zach Marrel, cover designer; pre-press, printing, and binding by the graphics division of Saint Mary's Press.

Printed in the United States of America

Printing: 9 8 7 6 5 4 3 2 1

Year: 2007 06 05 04 03 02 01 00 99

ISBN 0-88489-603-X

This storybook is dedicated to all of you whose stories are recorded here. It was a special privilege to talk with you. Some of you were strangers; now you have found a niche in my heart. Others of you have been a part of me over time and I am grateful; you have touched my life again. All of you have enriched me beyond measure.

One of the greatest gifts in my life has been this opportunity to spend time with you, each of us struggling to attain the purpose for which we have been created. May the Creator continue to claim all of us as God's children.

CONTENTS

Time for . . .

PREFACE

This is a storybook. It explores a time in life that each person has experienced. These are not fairy tales or legends, for each story is true. Each testifies to incidents that fostered or hindered growth. Neither are there duplicates, for even when individuals have similar experiences, their responses are unique.

Some stories are so simple and routine that we can identify with them immediately. Others are so traumatic and exceptional that they help us see life in ways previously foreign to us. They expand our understanding. They do not encourage imitation, but they can motivate us to live our life to the full.

The common thread weaving among the stories is the endeavor that persons make to live life fully in the circumstances in which they find themselves. People who have been in the public arena are identified. Most of the others are identified only by their first names. Some names are pseudonyms.

I trust that these stories will powerfully inspire you, help you connect with the common denominator of humanity, and give you courage—if you are hesitating—to raise to the surface some secret that you have kept hidden. May they inspire you to share your story with others and so recognize the meaning and depth it gives to you and to them.

INTRODUCTION

The Internet carried this anonymous article on time:

> Imagine there is a bank that credits your account each morning with $86,400 but carries over no balance from day to day, allows you to keep no cash, and every evening cancels whatever part of the account you had failed to use during the day. Everyone has such a bank, and it is called Time.
>
> Every morning Time credits you with 86,400 seconds. Every night it writes off, as lost, whatever you have failed to invest to good purpose. It allows no overdraft. Each day it opens a new account. Each night it burns the records of the day. If you fail to use the day's deposits, the failure is yours.
>
> There is no going back nor any drawing against "tomorrow." You must live in the present on today's deposits. Invest it so as to get from it the utmost in health, happiness, and success. The clock is running; make the most of today.
>
> To realize the value of one year, ask a student who has failed an exam.
>
> To realize the value of one month, ask a mother who has given birth to a premature baby.
>
> To realize the value of one week, ask an editor of a weekly newspaper.
>
> To realize the value of one day, ask a daily wage laborer who has ten kids to feed.
>
> To realize the value of one hour, ask the person who has missed a plane.
>
> To realize the value of one second, ask a person who has survived an accident.
>
> To realize the value of one millisecond, ask the person who has won a silver medal in the Olympics.

Time is a mystery, and no words can truly define it. We live in time, but really don't know what it is. We segment it into pieces: a past, a present, and a future. How do each of these connect?

The past is the moment that just passed, or it is yesterday or yesteryear that jerks us around spasmodically and disrupts the present, the moment that is now. Each swing of the pendulum reminds us of the mistakes, losses, failures, inadequacies, and fragmentation that no longer are present. Yet we are yoked to this past as if it were the primary reason for our present existence.

The future is that "tomorrow" for which we yearn. If we focus too much on the future, we are robbed of that which needs our attention in this moment, and when that moment comes, it too instantaneously becomes the past. So time is fleeting. Each moment moves inexorably forward, and we cannot stop it.

Even though we can move backward in time through memory and move forward through anticipation, every second hand, every minute hand, as they move, constitute the now. In the blink of an eye, the now becomes the past. If we are wise, we root ourselves in the now, using the present for learning, growth, and enjoyment in spite of the happenstance of the moment, for it too will pass away.

At times, time moves so slowly that we want to nudge it along. At other times it whizzes by, and we wish that we could grasp it and contain it, but it slides like jelly through our fingers.

Even though we cannot define it, time makes life possible. It allows for change. We see this in the rhythmic seasons that govern our activities and control our food supply. We recognize it in the rising and setting of the sun and in the moon cycles. Sea animals time their activities to the tides.

Plants, animals, and humans start with a seed and, in time, are gradually transformed into other forms. Humans are born, live through childhood, adolescence, midlife, maturity, and age. We mark these passages through time with various celebrations.

Time allows us to establish events in relation to other events, but we cannot live in an earlier time. Once events happen they cannot be cancelled, but their effects can be changed through subsequent actions. It is critical to realize this when we regret what we have said or done. Even though we cannot revoke our actions, in the now we can still change any destructive impact through forgiveness, reparation, and love. How wise is it to waste time being unhappy or bitter?

Each of us has stories of what we have become and accomplished in time. If we treasure personal stories, our autobiography can prove to be an inspiration for others. It can establish a link with both past and future generations. It can be a gift to others as they surface the common denominator of humanity.

T he idea for this book came in the middle of a summer night. The verses from Ecclesiastes 3:1–8 surfaced subconsciously, and I wondered what significance they had for me. It was while reflecting on them later that I could see how life is made up of many opportunities, numerous experiences, and varied responses.

Some of the times listed in Ecclesiastes may not touch our lives as significantly as they did in antiquity. We experience times today that are similar, but we also experience times that may have been unfamiliar to the people who lived when Ecclesiastes was written.

The ancient writer says:

For everything there is a season, and a time for every matter under heaven:
>   a time to be born, and a time to die;
>   a time to plant, and a time to pluck up what is planted;
>   a time to kill, and a time to heal;
>   a time to break down, and a time to build up;
>   a time to weep, and a time to laugh;
>   a time to mourn, and a time to dance;
>   a time to throw away stones, and a time to gather stones
>   together;
>   a time to embrace, and a time to refrain from embracing;
>   a time to seek, and a time to lose;
>   a time to keep, and a time to throw away;
>   a time to tear, and a time to sew;
>   a time to keep silence, and a time to speak;
>   a time to love, and a time to hate;
>   a time for war, and a time for peace.

Much of this is evident in contemporary times. Yet we have times that focus on different events and responses. Simple reflection reveals experiences that do not seem to be of consequence to the times of the ancient writer, but that do impinge on our life today. So, in addition to some of those listed in Ecclesiastes, I have included my limited inventory:

A time for God, and a time for joy;
a time for identity, and a time for acceptance;
a time for justice, and a time for forgiveness;
a time for grieving, and a time for transformation;
a time for searching, and a time for struggle;
a time for suffering, and a time for healing;
a time for eldering, and a time for wisdom;
a time for work, and a time for ministry;
a time for love, and a time for memories.

This observation surfaced questions for me. What is time? What happens to us in that period between our appearance and our disappearance in this thing we call time? Do all of us have similar or differing journeys as we move from a beginning to an end point? What happens to us on that continuum? How is our physical, emotional, and spiritual growth affected by the events occurring in the interim? Where is the spirit of God in time?

I began my exploration of our life-time by asking interesting, insightful people to tell stories about the times or seasons spoken of in Ecclesiastes. Surprised at the interest and enthusiasm with which individuals responded to my request for a story from their life, I felt like a vessel being filled with sweet wine. I have not experienced what some others have, but I have been strengthened by the visions I beheld: visions of struggle, suffering, enthusiasm, dedication, failure and success, love beyond measure, forgivenesss, transformation, and joy. They are a witness to the power of the Spirit.

Listening to and recording these stories brought to mind a dream I once had. A friend of mine had told me that in recurring dreams, he was standing at an abyss, fearful he might jump. One night my dream re-enacted his in some measure. I was standing in a meadow across a road. In front of me was a hill, and to its left, a tunnel. My friend was standing at the top of this hill, looking down into an abyss.

An impulse pulled me up that hill, and as I came up behind him, I shoved him over and then leaned out to see what would happen. Down below was a glorious figure with arms outstretched. My friend fell gently into them, and then both, standing upright with arms around each other's waist, walked into the tunnel. I raced down the hill and faced the tunnel, eager to see what would happen. There was no groaning, no light, no shouts of any kind. Soon my friend emerged alone from the mouth of the tunnel with a radiant smile and a buoyant step. I sensed that in that darkness his companion had lifted his burden.

This, it seems, is what is happening in the telling of these stories. Experiences have been raised to the light, bringing joy and peace in the knowledge that lives have been precious, God has been a guide, and our short span in time has meaning and influence. So, I share these stories of the times of people's lives—raised to the light for our comfort, challenge, inspiration, and guidance.

You will gain a deeper insight about humanity because of the sharing of the storytellers. They broaden our horizons. And, really, their story is our story, because they are part of the human story. Draw comfort, open your heart to understanding, rejoice in life as lived to the full by so many people in spite of obstacles, and join your spirit with the spirit of these storytellers. You can then accept the wisdom offered and gratefully own the wisdom gained through your own experiences.

What is time?
Is it a period, a point, an occasion when something or
someone exists?
Is it a moment or an hour when something commences, happens, or
culminates?

Why does time hang heavy on our hands?
Why does it move so slowly at times?
Why don't we have time to lose?
Where do we store the time we save?

When do we draw upon it?
Why do we waste time?
How do we discard it?

What does it mean to take time to love?
> to be present to someone?
> to communicate with God?

What is a lifetime?

Is it measured by chronicles, calendars, clocks?
When does it begin, achieve fullness, and end?
Do we live in Zulu time? solar time? daylight saving time?
How do instants and seconds,
> minutes and hours,
> days and weeks,
> months and years,
> decades and centuries

affect, enclose, and determine our lives?
Do we live within an era, an epoch, or an eon?

What's the timetable?

From time immemorial we are destined for birth, growth, and death.
We live until there has been time enough to be alone inside our skin,
to let the pendulum measure the sequence of our existence.
We have the time of our life and then our time is up.
The door opens upon eternity,
and time is one timeless present.
We stand before the Lord of time immersed in love,
and time stands still.

TIME FOR GOD

God is indeed a mystery, revealing Self in the ordinary events in our life. Our vocabulary is so limited and our imagination so confined that we cannot fully grasp nor understand this Presence. Yet we fumble as we search in faith to find certainty in God's existence.

We are claimed by material possessions and susceptible to that which gives us pleasure. We reject pain and rebel against Jesus' call to take up our daily crosses. We live as if we will exist on Earth forever. We renounce the surrender that can enfold us in blessed and loving arms. The call to become God-like frightens us, but we trust that in opening ourselves, God can nourish in us the seeds of the Creator's likeness. God's time is all time.

News of the mutilated bodies of a woman and two children found near the Guatemalan border reached Roberto five years after their death. Roberto finally knew that his family had been killed. The man who had waited to lead Roberto's family out of El Salvador found Roberto's wife's body and removed the ring from her finger. When it was safe to do so, he sent it to Roberto, whose name was engraved inside it.

The death of his family completed the circle of anguish that had begun for Roberto years before, when President Napoleon Duarte had asked him to go undercover to investigate the activities of the death squads and the atrocities of the military. After finding sufficient evidence about them, including their murder of the four American women who had been killed in December 1980, and their assassination of Archbishop Oscar Romero earlier that year, Roberto presented his evidence. He also reported what he had witnessed during Romero's funeral while standing on the steps of the cathedral. The National

Guard had fired their machine guns and rifles into the crowd in the plaza.

Duarte now asked Roberto to investigate the confrontation between the military and the guerrillas near the city of San Miguel. Upon arrival Roberto witnessed soldiers collecting I.D. tags and fingerprints or footprints of their own dead. A sergeant confided that the military chiefs, upon proving that the men were dead, collected on the dead soldiers' insurance policies, giving their families only the amount to cover the funerals. Before Roberto's eyes the bodies were burned in a mass grave.

Duarte refused to make the evidence public because it was so damaging. He feared that the military would turn on him. But Roberto had nightmares of dismembered bodies, the wailing of the relatives, and the nauseating smell of the dead.

One day sometime later, as he went jogging with his security guards, Roberto glanced through the slightly opened door to the basement of the hotel where he was living. Upon investigation the joggers discovered a large cache of weapons in boxes labeled "U.S. Government." He reported the incident and was told not to worry about it.

At midnight two weeks later, Roberto watched as several large trucks arrived filled with soldiers. A car followed them, and from it several colonels and an intelligence chief alighted. The hotel owner joined them. To Roberto's amazement two guerrillas appeared, and one of the colonels accepted envelopes from them and openly counted the money. Then the guerrillas packed the ammunition into their own trucks and drove off.

Roberto could no longer keep quiet, even though Duarte felt helpless. When he began talking about what he had discovered, the death threats started. Duarte refused to call a news conference. So in November 1982, Roberto gave the conference. Fearing for their families, the reporters refused to publish the documentation.

Not long after, the National Police stormed into his office and arrested Roberto. If he retracted what he had told the reporters, confessed to spying for the guerrillas, and denounced his brother and nephews as guerrillas, he would be given his freedom. All he had to do was to sign a confession. If not, he would die. Roberto refused to sign. If he was to die, he would die with dignity.

Roberto languished in prison without trial from November 1982 through June 1986. The guards tortured him steadily. They broke his teeth and yanked out the gold fillings. They broke his hands and hung him by his neck, permanently damaging his Adam's apple. Several times they pulled a rubber hood filled with caustic substances over his head to induce suffocation. He vomited blood and lost consciousness.

One day his tormentors stretched him spread-eagle between two columns, then doused him in cold water prior to applying hot electrical wires to his body. They threatened to castrate him.

During this torture Roberto saw a young man dressed in a red tunic standing before him. His face was bloody and scarred, and his radiant head was crowned with thorns. Gazing at Roberto, he extended his hand to Roberto, who was filled with a warm glow that anesthetized his pain. Roberto wondered if he was dying, and asked forgiveness from the vision.

Roberto survived, and was soon transferred to another prison, where he spent eighteen months in isolation. A visitor again urged him to sign the "documents." When he again refused, he was subjected to psychological tortures: mock executions every other evening for ninety days, a guard regularly firing his gun at or around the door of his cell. Roberto was taken to see the bodies of others who were tortured. He estimates that he saw at least one hundred cadavers. He was also forced to witness guards raping the young male prisoners.

Roberto's case was finally heard by a tribunal at the end of May 1986. Unable to find evidence for the accusations of conspiracy against the government, selling arms to the guerrillas, or of being a guerrilla, the military court declared him innocent of the charges. He was released.

Roberto arrived in the United States after a torturous journey through Mexico. At the end he had collapsed on the edge of the Arizona desert and was found by a compassionate resident who gave him asylum. The Center for Victims of Torture accepted him for physical and psychological treatment.

Roberto still suffers from his experiences. Yet he bears no hatred, nor does he desire revenge on his torturers. The pain and grief he feels for his murdered family has not made him bitter. But he is not silent about the injustices that he witnessed. Even though he still gets periodic death threats, he has testified in the U.S. Congress. Due in part to his testimony, the U.S. government cut military aid to El Salvador from one and a half million dollars a day to twenty-two million dollars a year. President Bush also forced the Salvadoran military to reach agreement with the guerrillas. The image of that compassionate Man's visit to Roberto's cell has given him the power to survive, to forgive, to continue.

Who are you, God?
I am the power that strengthens,
the power of grace,
investing you with the ability
to withstand all odds.

God means everything to me." Aleida is convinced that the events in her life are truly a blessing of God's presence. She can enumerate many examples.

One of seven children born in Minnesota after her parents migrated from the Netherlands, Aleida grew up on a farm. This life brought her close to God, as did the stories from the children's Bible her mother read to her. In addition to the Bible stories, she was particularly impressed by Jo and her home in the novel Little Women.

Aleida always felt God's presence in her life, but never really understood what that meant. So in 1938, searching for an anchor for her faith, she joined the Lutheran church. Her husband did not belong to any particular faith but went church hopping.

Her dream of having a home like Jo's began to materialize. Unable to have children, the couple became foster parents. Gradually the house filled up with tiny babies, toddlers, runaways, and abandoned youngsters. They became brothers and sisters in a family that loved them. Some of the thirty-seven foster children still live close to Aleida.

As a teen Aleida had wanted to write poetry, but never got around to it until her husband's death in 1984. This first poem she entitled "Our First Christmas Without Dad":

My family gathers again this year,
but there's a vacant chair.
Dad is no longer here with us,
a sadness we all share.

We didn't know on this day last year
that heaven was just weeks away.
If he could whisper in our ears,
he'd say, "Have happy thoughts today."

So may we all this merry day
keep smiling as we gather here,
keep faith in God, have trust in God,
our father's home we'll someday share.

Despite the faith expressed in the poem, Aleida grew depressed. One day as she was tearfully praying, she clearly heard: "Sure, you can survive; just take one step at a time. God will be with you." Later when she visited her doctor, he told her to walk whenever she was depressed.

She pleaded with God to give her something worthwhile to do with her life. Then one day while watching television, she heard a man recruiting walkers for a 3,500-mile trek across America to promote world peace and nuclear disarmament. She decided to become one of the walkers.

Aleida's foster children pitched in the money she needed, but there were those who were sure it was folly for her to attempt such a challenge at age sixty-eight. Nevertheless she set off for Los Angeles to begin the walk.

A month after the walkers began, they ran out of funds and were advised to return home. Although nine hundred people left, three hundred were determined to complete the walk. Camp vehicles transported them to several large cities where they solicited funds house-to-house. The publicity drew hundreds of new walkers.

Aleida admits: "The eight-and-a-half-month journey was rough. One time we were stranded in the desert for twelve days, and I spent two weeks on crutches because of infections in my feet." She was hit by a car and spent two days in a motel recovering from her bruises. "In spite of all this, I will never forget the scenery, especially the mountains where I felt like a pebble on a beach. Our trip was just like life, full of surprises."

By the time the walkers reached Washington, D.C., their ranks had swelled to seven thousand five hundred. People from other countries joined them. "The best part of finishing was hearing the church bells that greeted us as we entered the city."

That one walk wasn't enough. At the age of seventy-two, Aleida walked from Albuquerque, New Mexico, to Washington, D.C., this time to draw attention to environmental issues. She plans no other walks, but is writing a book about her experiences so that her foster children and grandchildren will remember her. She also gives talks to dispel stereotypes about aging.

"Time was given me to keep living life fully. In spite of what happens, I need to respond to it wholeheartedly, regardless of the challenges. The Lord has been with me all along, and God will not abandon me now or in the future."

Who are you, God?
Presence, always faithful, my confidant, companion.
Unreserved acceptance,
treasuring me in spite of weakness,
challenging me to greatness.

Panic! That's what set in when Mary was told that, after nearly a third of a century in electronic media, the firm was being downsized and she would need to leave. She had taken real pride in having worked steadily and loyally for several radio and TV stations from the month after graduation to that day in 1985 when it came to an end.

Over the years Mary had written countless pieces of television copy whose end was generally indicated by the words, "Go to black." With the curtain closing on her longtime career, Mary "went to black" herself. She plunged into desolation. Never having married, she had always rowed her own canoe through treacherous financial waters. She had never made a lot of money, but she always had enough to ride out the monetary storms she encountered from time to time.

This was different. At the time, Mary was nearly fifty-five years old and ill-prepared to retire. Where would she find a source of adequate income in her community? Moving from Montana was not an option. Her ninety-three-year-old mother, who had been a nursing-home patient for three years, was failing rapidly and was entirely dependent upon her. Where would she find the necessary resources to continue her mother's care without a spouse, children, or siblings?

Then, as if to underscore the urgency of the situation, Mary's mother suffered a massive stroke. "It was then I dropped all pretense of being self-sufficient and turned to God. It was time for my rock-bottom prayer, a term I had coined years earlier for those occasions when my human resources had run out. I had no choice but to place myself and my situation totally in the hands of God."

Mary pleaded: "Here I am, God, fresh out of options. You know the situation, so there is no need to belabor that. I've come today to let you know that I am not simply interested in your help. We're way beyond that. You can scarcely help me do something when I haven't the least notion what to do. You are going to have to take over this dilemma with a capital, bold-faced D. I surrender, and I'll do my best to follow your lead. You'll have to be crystal clear, or I'll probably wander down the wrong path."

A gentle peace settled over Mary. She quit running around in tight circles and began handling each crisis as it arose. She knew that her rock-bottom prayer was not a license to mark time in her recliner, waiting for a certified letter from God. Quite the contrary. She followed every lead, investigated every possibility, mailed letters of inquiry, and answered classified ads for jobs, some of which she prayed she wouldn't get.

Weeks passed. Mary's financial resources dwindled at an alarming rate, and she seemed no closer to a new position. Then, two-and-a-half months into her desert experience, her mother died. She remembers thinking: "It's always darkest before the dawn. I should be seeing traces of light creeping into the eastern sky any minute."

Actually, the sun burst in full-dress regalia. In a single week, two phone calls changed the course of Mary's life. She was offered two positions, neither of which she had applied for. One was as director of religious education (DRE) on a parish staff. The other was a teaching position in the religious-studies department of a Catholic high school.

Having had several months to absorb the desirability of a paycheck, she took both offers.

Mary's master's degree in religious studies qualified her for both new ventures, but she had no experience. Undaunted, she continued life with two new careers. She also continued her freelance writing and adult education classes. Even though she wondered if she could juggle all these commitments, Mary was convinced that this was an overwhelming reply to her rock-bottom prayer. "I determined to give it everything I had, using my God-given arsenal of gifts and talents, privileges and abilities."

Mary's first year was like wandering through a maze blindfolded, bumping into unforeseen obstacles. In June, at the end of the academic year, she found that she had not only survived but was happier than she had ever been. "I was in a niche that fit me perfectly. I loved teaching about God, especially to young adults, and quickly developed a tremendous admiration for and relationship with remarkable young people."

After eleven exciting, fulfilling years, Mary opted to discontinue teaching. "It was one of the most difficult decisions of my life. I knew I would miss the classroom and the young people who made it such an exciting place, but it was time to move on."

Even though she continues writing and lecturing, Mary acknowledges that the long-term direction of her life is shrouded, and she can't see far ahead. "When the uncertainty starts making me nervous, I press 'rewind' on my memory video and return to those harrowing months when I turned my life over to God and received, in return, the most glorious years I've ever known."

"To me age is merely a number for all of us, young and old. Even though some may think I am 'over the hill,' neither God nor I see it that way. Some terrific years are still before me, maybe even the best. I have time to build new spiritual edifices. I can hardly wait."

God, who are you?
Peace, tranquillity, harmony,
calming the churning waters in my heart,
soothing turmoil and uncertainty.

Gently reconciling, pouring balm upon my wounds,
healing my shattered fragments.

I s it compassion or is it justice? When Solomon made the decision to cut the baby in half, did he really know that the rightful mother would surrender the right to her child so that it might live? What risk did Solomon take in seeking justice?

The same questions could have been asked of Judge Patrick Fitzgerald when he decided to bypass the recommended sentence for an African American male who had shot off a gun. Or when he refused to allow an African American woman who had stolen expensive furs in Minneapolis to return to Illinois to serve out her sentence.

After a softball game, Malcum, in his early twenties, went with the rest of his teammates to a bar to socialize. Racial epithets were aimed at Malcum. Finally, when someone called him "black Sambo," he left the bar, went home, got a gun, and returned. As he fired a shot in the air, he shouted, "Now I'll teach you a thing or two."

Malcum was arrested and charged with felony assault. The jury found him guilty. According to the sentencing guidelines, the use of a gun mandated at least three years in prison. Judge Fitzgerald sensed that three years behind bars would turn the young man into a hardened criminal. He decided to revoke the sentence.

The judge's decision overrode the objections of the county attorney and the probation officer. Eventually they agreed on a sentence of five years on probation under strict supervision. Malcum could not drink or take drugs and would be subject to periodic urinalysis. He could possess no weapons, have no law violations, and had to find employment. He had to report bimonthly to his probation officer.

At the end of the first year, Malcum was back before Judge Fitzgerald to report that he had a good job and was engaged. After his second year, he brought his wife and baby and told of his promotion at work. At the end of the fifth year, he expressed his gratitude for the judge's mercy. It had turned his life around.

Judge Fitzgerald knew he had made the right decision, for the totality of the circumstances presented in court had indicated injustice.

Malcum's background check had detailed that he was clean and held the promise of a good future.

The second case was different. Sasha, a professional shoplifter, had come from Chicago with orders from her bosses to return with fur coats. She stole two coats worth ten thousand dollars, was arrested, and was sentenced by Judge Fitzgerald to one year in the women's workhouse.

Chicago aldermen pressured the judge to return Sasha there to be tried for another crime. The judge sensed that their request was an attempt to free her. He notified the aldermen that she could be tried in Chicago after her time in Minneapolis was served.

In three years Sasha was back before the judge, bearing gifts. "I am grateful you were tough and held to your decision," she said, "for it gave me time to reflect on my past life. I was able to project what I would be like if I continued stealing. My incarceration changed the direction of my life and my family." The judge was happy to hear that she had turned her life around, but graciously refused the gifts.

Judge Fitzgerald is convinced he could not make sound judgments without the help of the Spirit. Daily prayer and the Eucharist prepare him for the tasks of the day.

By the time of his retirement, Judge Fitzgerald had given forty-six years of his life to the justice system as a practicing lawyer, teacher of law, and municipal court judge. He recognizes that judges have great power that they can use in assisting people who appear in court to reassess their lives. "Although there are a few judges who are influenced by circumstances or status rather than by truth, they are in the minority. My goal was to empower those who came before me to learn from their mistakes and change their lives. It did not always happen, but when it did, it brought much satisfaction."

Who are you, God?
Justice sorrowing for wrongdoers,
calling them to repentance,
seeking the impenitent, granting them amnesty,
tempering their hardheartedness with mercy.

John Simkins offered this response to the question, Who are you, God?

The air is still cool but the snow is almost gone.
The sidewalks glisten with the melt.
I've come to be with You.
As usual, it is a quiet affair,
a space where nothing happens,
a space where whole worlds come into existence,
grow, age, and whither away,
a space where there is no time.

The lights of the skyline burn without talking:
just candles, just pain, just wounds.
Your silence reminds me that I need not explain.
You already know.
Your silence allows me a moment
in which to open up my anger and my grief.
Your silence is big enough to swallow them up.
Your voice becomes my silence.

Traffic is persistent,
as if lost souls are searching the night
for the home they misplaced along the river,
or perhaps across the bridge or up the hill.
For me it does no good
to seek inside and out.
You always laugh because after all this time,
I still have a tendency to miss the point.

If I just walk and be,
keep quiet,
just walk and be,
You are there,
inside and out, all around.

I lift my head to see,
or try to grasp,
and, there, I've missed the point again.

I sit on a bench a while
amid the bottomless dark static
of the urban night.
I gaze stupidly
past this world of meaningless ferment,
this world so extraneous to me now.
I have this secret that I tell no one,
no one at all.

We have been together again tonight.
I was lost in Your grasp;
I swam in the exquisite nothingness of Your smile;
I bled out into the silver gray night.
Then I disappeared for a time
for there was only You.

TIME FOR BIRTH

God's eternal mind holds everything, including humankind, in its dominion in ways we cannot comprehend. Because we are, then we have always been a part of the spirit of God. Certain gifts and talents, responses, and behaviors identify us as unique, although all of us have one common characteristic: we are the children of God.

Just as we exist in God's mind, so we now exist on Earth in the span of time allotted to us. We have a journey to take that will lead us back to that eternal now. God remains the mentor, always available during our duration here.

From the moment we are conceived, our life-clock begins, and we begin to age. Even the months we spend in the womb are numbered, and as we leave it, we begin to tick off the months and years and decades. We move forward to the time when we will return to our Creator. But always there is a time for birth.

Joe Germann was reading a biography about a woman who was pregnant and had breast cancer. Her doctor told her that the hormonal shifts accompanying her pregnancy would act like a fertilizer for any cancer cells in her body, for her tumor was estrogen positive. It was possible that neither she nor her child would survive. The couple wanted to have the baby, but the doctor advised an abortion. In great agony they followed the doctor's recommendation.

After reading this story, Joe had a new understanding of his father's and mother's love for him. His father was a surgeon. He had survived World War I and had started a medical practice in Los Angeles. He fell in love and married Beatrice. Together they started a family with two sons, Albert and Thomas. Then Beatrice contracted cancer, which systematically destroyed the hopes and dreams of a young family. Beatrice left behind two small children and a heartbroken husband.

Years passed, and Joe's father fell in love with Winifred, a social worker for the Catholic church. Winifred returned that love by embracing the two young boys as well. The family was whole and growing again. She gave birth to Timothy. A year later Winifred was pregnant again. It was now Joe's turn to enter the world. Expectations were high.

However, just as in the biography Joe was reading, his mother was diagnosed with breast cancer. Both parents were aware of the possible medical consequences. Winifred, wife and mother of three small boys, could die, and the baby with her. A decision had to be made.

Even though he had lost his first wife to cancer, Joe's father agreed with Winifred to give the child in her womb a chance at life. Winifred died six months after Joe's birth. Of course as a child, Joe could never comprehend what his mother had done for him, and no one had ever mentioned the heartaches generated during that last year of Winifred's life.

Later, reflecting on the choice she had made, Joe recognized that his mother had literally died for him. "My mother was a great soul. She took on a ready-made family and gave it all the love she had. She gave up her life for me."

Such love became an energizing force for Joe. He earned a degree in science and a master's degree in theology. He went back to school to get a teacher's certificate to teach fifth graders. In between his studies, he served as a pilot in the United States Air Force. Joe served as a lay theologian in Catholic parishes and then was ordained a deacon. Now he is a volunteer chaplain in a local hospital and a prison, and he heads the Ministerial Alliance Association in Winnsboro, Texas.

Joe is proud of Mary, his wife, and their six children. "Five of them have graduated from college, two with master's degrees. All are independent and successful and have given Mary and me grandchildren, who are an additional joy." He also acknowledges: "All of this was possible because of my mother's great love. My mother is a model of courage for me. She not only gave me life but also left a legacy challenging me to live to the fullest the life she gave me."

O Holy One,
in my mother's womb
you fashioned me a home.
My skin is the tent
protecting all that is within.
The furnishings are priceless:
gifts, talents, skills, abilities, and yearnings.
I am your temple, O God.
Because I am precious in your eyes,
you set up your reign
deep, deep in the core of my being.
O Holy One,
may I never separate myself from you,
or force you to leave the premises of my spirit.
My home is yours.
Abide within me forever.

TIME FOR PLANTING

Each of us is born from a seed implanted in a fertile womb. All seeds, of course, produce only their own kind. A watermelon seed cannot produce oranges. An oak seed cannot create a poplar.

Yet there are other kinds of seeds whose fruitfulness cannot be determined. Attitudes, words, values, and actions are seeds that we plant in the human heart. We hope these seeds will ripen into blossoms of beauty, spreading a sweet fragrance.

We are both planters and receivers of the seed. How fertile and yielding is the soil of our hearts? What is it we plant in the hearts of others in our time of planting?

Tom Jennings, mayor of Roswell, New Mexico, from 1994 to 1998, enjoyed what fleeting glory went with the position. During his tenure he met President Clinton, the mayors of other cities, sports figures, and national and international visitors. He formed the task force that organized the commemoration of the arrival of the unidentified flying object (UFO) that, according to Roswell's citizens, landed outside the city in 1947. That fiftieth anniversary in 1997 brought worldwide recognition. Thousands of visitors flocked to the city and the UFO museum.

Even so, Tom hadn't wanted to run for office when he was first recruited. His twin brother served in the New Mexico state legislature. Tom had decided that one politician in the family was enough. Nevertheless, the people of Roswell wanted new blood. Even though Tom was a Democrat and Roswell was strongly Republican, his election made it clear that new ideas were welcome.

Tom brought to the office values formed from the lessons of his father and from Saint Peter's, the school he had attended in Roswell.

He also brought skills from his higher education: marketing and management from Creighton University in Omaha and petroleum management from the University of Texas.

His election as mayor gave him political authority, and Tom's mission now was to empower as many of his constituents as possible and to open government up to the public. This vision became his guide.

Tom planted the seeds of a youthful evolution. He recognized that young people were frustrated with nothing to do and with no vision of future opportunities. So he formed a youth council and organized a town hall for youth. He also established a Character Counts! Council, emphasizing ethics and values such as responsibility, truthfulness, caring, respect, citizenship, and fairness. A daytime curfew was imposed, one of the first in the nation. Preventing truancy became a priority. Tom knew that if children were in school, they could not be in harm's way on the streets.

While working with Reach 2000, a local youth organization, Tom was able to secure grants and equipment, following up on the ideas suggested by youths. A teen center was established. He formed teen task forces that focused on school, family, recreation, and other youth issues.

All this emphasis on young people stirred some hostility from the establishment people. Nevertheless Tom accomplished most of what he had set out to do, and so, satisfied, he declared that one term was enough. Because he had a growing family, the obligations of night meetings and of being on constant call caused him to re-evaluate his priorities. In addition, the fifteen-thousand-dollar-a-year salary could not pay the bills.

"To achieve personal goals," says Tom, "one must have strong convictions in order to persevere. Critical also is the willingness to sacrifice in order to accomplish the tasks at hand. At this point in my life, I was given the opportunity to plant the seeds of good citizenship and moral integrity. I may not see what I have planted come to fruition, but I continue to trust that achievement and personal worth will flourish if one tends to the goals one has set."

A seed carrying the pattern
of what it is to be,

> whether planted in the heart or in the earth,
> must find a welcoming embrace.
> Its fertilization and growth
> depend upon the care it's given.
> Pregnant with its power to produce,
> it lies fallow,
> waiting for the opportune time
> for the maturation of its fruitfulness.

Madonna's brother was a brilliant, witty, and handsome alcoholic who was in and out of correctional facilities. He committed suicide in his home when he was thirty-two. Madonna wondered whether the suicide could have been avoided if there had been compassionate people to encourage and support him.

So for over two decades, Madonna has been a volunteer working in the federal, state, and county corrections facilities in South Dakota, Alabama, and Minnesota. Through a weekly seminar, "Healthy, Positive Thinking," Madonna helps inmates realize that they need to make choices to make a difference in their lives. Most of all Madonna wants to show the inmates that God loves them and gives them hope to find a purpose for their lives: to give them the gift that her brother never received.

Madonna also helps conduct Charis, a weekend program facilitated by an ecumenical team of women and men. The inmates commit themselves to the full weekend. They have a series of talks, small-group discussions. They sing, pray, and participate in a reconciliation and worship service. Madonna claims: "It is an experience touching their hearts deeply. Often inmates come to the weekend so disabled by fear and self-loathing, it is hard for them to accept God's forgiveness and to forgive themselves."

Another purpose of Charis—to Christianize the prison environment through the inmates' words and behavior—is also achieved after the weekend. This is done by forming small prayer groups that meet weekly, with participants accountable to one another. They question each other about what each is doing to make the prison a more

Christlike environment. The process helps them bond with and trust one another as they take time to sow seeds that can bear fruit when they leave.

The Charis team returns monthly for follow-up. At this meeting a single inmate shares with a single team member what he or she is doing to make the prison a better place.

Madonna received the Franciscan International Award, but she makes light of it. "Being in the company of such distinguished people as Billy Graham, Dr. Charles Mayo, journalist Harry Reasoner, and the staff of *Sesame Street* is an honor, but I look to Saint Francis and Mother Teresa as models."

Madonna recognizes that she may not see the results of her efforts, but trusts that the seed planted will bring forth its fruit in due season. "All of us are our brothers' and sisters' keepers. We have to reach out to support and encourage one another."

Without nurture and cultivation,
seeds shrivel up and die,
never bringing to fruition
what they could have been.

TIME FOR SUFFERING

Suffering is an evil, although it can have redemptive results. No one is exempt from suffering in some form or the other. We sometimes reproach God for allowing pain to dominate or to surface in our life. The questioning we do and the resentment we feel are not fruitless if they help us learn something about ourselves, God, and the world.

To accept suffering when all other avenues have been explored may lead us to the understanding needed to surmount our pain. This understanding can then be extended to others who are in pain.

Suffering is not a punishment, nor is it the will of God. It happens because of a weakness in our body, mind, heart, or spirit. Or we may suffer because of an infirmity in our neighbor who vents displeasure or hatred on us. Then, too, accidents inflict unexpected pain that leads either to capitulation, to self-pity, or to determined survival.

Jesus healed those who sincerely believed he had that power. Jesus calls all his followers to heal. If pain is unavoidable, we can follow the example of our Savior's courage, patience, and faithfulness when he too suffered hunger, fatigue, betrayal, accusations, misunderstanding, and misrepresentations. Then the time of suffering becomes a time for transformation.

While eating licorice as she watched a children's program, Diane had a brain hemorrhage. She hasn't eaten it since. When the ambulance arrived to take her to the hospital, the family physician, who lived a few blocks away, insisted on going with her. Some well-honed instinct led him to perform a spinal tap as soon as they arrived at the hospital. Her parents credit him with saving Diane's life, because the procedure released the pressure in her head and began the brain's healing process.

While in surgery Diane had an out-of-body experience. She saw herself lying on the table in an operating room with seven medical personnel surrounding her. She still has a clear picture of herself looking down on everyone. Several days later an Asian woman doctor came to visit her, and Diane recognized her as one of the people who had been in the operating room.

The experience removed all Diane's fear of death. "I consider this to be one of the luckiest experiences I have had. I know I don't have to take it on faith because I learned that who I am is separate from my body. I am also convinced that God spared me for a particular reason, because not too many people survive a brain hemorrhage, even today."

Diane's parents had been told that what had occurred was like a "birthmark" on the brain, and the chances of it occurring again were slim. Yet forty years later, Diane began having dizzy spells. An MRI test destroyed the theory of the birthmark. She had an arterial vascular malformation (AVM). An angiogram confirmed the diagnosis. Surgery was recommended.

Diane put off surgery for three months because she would not have healed enough to attend a week-long seminar completing her training program to do spiritual direction. As the date for surgery neared, she became anxious, and she and Tom, her husband, decided to discuss their concerns with the neurosurgeon.

"When the surgeon walked in," says Diane, "I sensed an immediate feeling of peace. The first words he said were, 'You don't have to have this surgery immediately. If you have lived with the AVM for forty years, you can probably survive another year.'"

The doctor's change of mind stunned them and caused Diane to view many things differently. One important change was in her relationship with her mother. For years they had been unable to talk about her childhood experience. During all the weeks of Diane's illness and recovery, her mother had been terrified, but had stifled her fears. Indeed, she seemed to grow detached. For her part Diane wondered why her mother had been so emotionally distant. Now forty years old, Diane opened up to her mother, who shared that fear had closed communication. Now some of the pain in both hearts has healed.

"This health issue has put to rest all apprehensions about my future, for all I have is today," says Diane. "From the day this crisis began, I was open to whatever God had to teach me. I consider each day of my present journey a gift, for in these short months, I learned what might have taken me a lifetime to learn."

Diane filled her gratitude journal with entries about all those who prayed for and supported her, the understanding of her family, and the doctor's affirmation of her decision. "It was a grace-filled time. I am sure of God's love, and sense that I can trust God, no matter what happens in the future."

Suffering has the power
to destroy our wholeness.
But it can overpower us only
when we are numbed, resentful, impatient, angry,
and we give it such control.
When suffering takes on meaning,
it ceases to be suffering,
becoming a redemptive sacrifice,
breaking our restless hearts open,
allowing compassion an entrance.

At five years old, Beverly would get down on her hands and knees to push Uncle Hal's feet as he moved forward with his cane. Today she visits him in an assisted-living home where he is bedridden, unable to walk at all.

For a man who flew transport planes during World War II and played saxophone and guitar in the big bands of the era, lying flat on his back paralyzed by multiple sclerosis (MS) could easily be a disaster. But it isn't so for Harold. "I am blessed I am not worse than I am. Lying in bed helps me keep things in perspective."

Harold was born in Oak Park, Illinois, as World War I was ending. In school, music was his passion, and he became proficient with several instruments. He played in the high school band, and when he graduated, he immediately found a job with a band. His travels began. Playing in Chicago, San Diego, Saint Paul, and New York put him in touch with big-band players across the country. Life was good and full of promise.

Then Pearl Harbor intervened. In 1942, at age twenty-four, Harold volunteered for the Air Force. After training he was sent to New Caledonia in the Pacific to transport troops to and from the beaches. He barely escaped with his life during the Japanese attacks on his plane.

Paralysis began in Harold's early thirties, claiming his ankles first. He felt no pain as it crept up his legs to affect his bladder. In 1949 he went to Hines Veterans Hospital outside of Chicago to be diagnosed. Once the verdict was MS, life changed drastically. By the early 1950s, he was totally immobilized. "I was upset, but actually all I could do was depend on the doctors, pray, trust God to give me patience, and roll with the punches."

Harold lived at home until his sister, his caregiver, died of cancer. His niece, his only living relative, helped him move to Saint Paul. She promised that he would not be put into a nursing home. Harold sold his home and prepared his will.

After six years, Harold's niece decided that she could not care for him at her home. So on Easter Sunday, against his wishes, Harold was moved into an assisted-living home. He has a private nurse, and his niece visits him frequently. In his wheelchair he can attend social events and, periodically, go to the dining room for meals.

"At first I felt uprooted, and accused my niece of not keeping her promise. But now I am accustomed to it and actually like it. I have forgiven her."

On the wall above Harold's bed is a crucifix, entwined by a rosary. "It is a constant reminder of Jesus' love for me, even in my inactivity. I don't want to suffer, but I am convinced that somehow my helplessness becomes a power, even though I don't quite understand how that happens.

"When I think of how Jesus suffered for me, then it is easier to become a victorious sufferer for others. I too am part of the mystical Body of Christ, and recognize that other parts of that body can be strengthened because I am spiritually healthy."

What good is suffering
when razor-sharp pain damages the fabric of the body
and hacks away at soul and spirit?
How difficult it is to understand God's love in this.

Yet after denial makes way for acceptance,
the way is made ready for faith, growth, and surrender.

After her regular mammogram and a biopsy, Jeanette discovered that her right breast was cancerous and needed to be removed. Denial, anger, and agitation rocked her. When she regained some measure of peace, she bought a rose, put it in the most beautiful vase she had, and wrote a poem.

> I bought a Rose for my right breast,
> a beautiful, long-stemmed Rose.
> My breast deserved it.
> It has been cut and bruised,
> and soon it will be gone for good.
>
> The tissues are healing well from the biopsy,
> just in time to be cut away for good
> through the mastectomy.
> This is the price of alcohol, too much fat,
> lots of stress, and genetics.
>
> My Rose is a metaphor for good-bye.
> I figure if I can separate in my mind
> my right breast from ME,
> I can let go of that piece I have known,
> that piece of me for almost fifty years,
> without letting go of ME.
>
> Good-bye, beautiful breast,
> be accompanied on your final platter
> with this Rose,
> this Rose of love,
> this Rose of ME.

Three days later Jeanette found out that her left breast was also cancerous and would need to be removed. The agonizing and questioning repeated itself. Now she needed a second rose. Another poem followed.

Oh no! What is this?
I need another Rose.
More cancer in my left breast.
How can this be?
How can a woman bear this news?

My breasts flowed and bounced with me
for so many years.
How can they simply be cut off?
A numbing sensation overwhelms me;
the biopsy can't be right!
I really can't accept the news,
not just yet.

In surrender I realize that another Rose,
another reverent symbol, will be lost.
After some tearful moments,
I turn to my higher power, my God.

A sense of serenity encompasses me.
I realize I was never in control.
I will have what I need,
for I must accept what I cannot change.
Peace embraces me.
'Tis the Rose of peace.

With the surgery scheduled within a week, Jeanette continued to struggle, fearful of the follow-up. Her life seemed a paradox. Facing the present and fearing the future were bouncing her on a teeter-totter. The shocking news settled in, and there was no turning back. Both breasts and two roses would die. Jeanette had adopted the Indian ritual of placing a burden on a selected flower, allowing the flower to die with that burden. She no longer watered the roses, and they responded with wilted petals.

Other wilting episodes intruded: the lost film from the mammogram, the short-tempered doctor who offered a second opinion, mounting medical expenses, and lack of money for medical treatments already completed.

Jeanette wanted to let go, but held on to some fears. So she prayed, "Take my breasts, but I can't handle chemo."

Even so, love and life surrounded Jeanette. Her daughters made close connections with her, a priest gave healing wisdom, and the loving voice of Ed, a close friend, embraced her. Nevertheless surgery confronted her.

"It is my Advent then," Jeanette recalls. "Tomorrow I walk to the cross with my buddy, Jesus." Before she went she bought two small rosebuds as a final tribute to the surgical journey. Her mind rallied around visions of resurrection, fresh roses, and prostheses.

After surgery Jeanette was greeted with a surprise. The cancer had not spread to the lymph nodes. No further treatment was necessary. Jeanette returned to work after a week. She had grieved within and mourned without for the death of a part of her body.

The grieving and mourning had taught Jeanette that obstacles could be overcome. "I have survived because I have a powerful advocate in Jesus, my buddy. His spirit keeps me strong."

In God's embrace suffering never
speaks the last word.
Holding on to God,
we learn compassion.
Suffering gives us courage
to invite the human God to suffer along with us.

TIME FOR HEALING

Pain can strike fast, devastate, lay waste to energy, trust, endeavor, and hope. On the other hand, healing seems to creep along languorously, appearing to hold us hostage to misery and despair. The road to healing demands patient endurance and a determination to survive.

It takes a second to slip and fall on the ice, but from six to eight weeks for a broken bone to heal. The arthritis that might follow may never heal. It takes a smattering of hate, jealousy, or judgment to sever the relationship with an individual made in God's image, but it takes repentance, acknowledgment of sin, and humility for reconciliation to heal the damage.

Within us is the well from which we can draw the reinforcements we need to heal, even when we need the help of physicians, counselors, spiritual guides, or friends. During a time of healing, these sources, united with the power of God, effect a powerful return to wholeness.

Bernadette submerged the trauma of her childhood deep within her psyche. Only after passing midlife did she begin having nightmares that awakened memories she didn't want to face: her mouth, hands, and feet tied with duct tape, she is locked in a two-by-three-foot closet for hours; a boarder in her home sets her free only to rape and abuse her. Or her mother beats her with the cat-o'-nine-tails, stripping her back. Rage overwhelms her mother and she stabs her other daughter with a knife. Bernadette is only ten years old.

Bernadette lands in the hospital, her back slashed so badly that she has to lie on her stomach. Pillows are placed on both sides of her so the sheets and blankets won't touch the open wounds. After some time has passed, she is turned on her back.

"It was then I found myself floating toward the ceiling, watching two African American nurses care for me. A calm filled me, and I saw how startled they were when the monitor indicated I was dying. I wanted to stay where I was, looking down at the nurses, the doctors, and a detective who never left my bedside. The medical personnel were trying to revive me. I didn't want to return, but they brought me back."

Other scenes in that kaleidoscope of traumatic memories are filled with terror. Bernadette's maternal grandfather raped her at the request of her mother. Because her mother couldn't bear any more children, she wanted to have them through Bernadette, who gave birth to twins at the age of thirteen.

"The irony was I couldn't keep the twins because I was underage. Mother couldn't get them because she was abusive. When I was released from Mercy-Douglas Hospital with my children, I was taken to a home for unwed mothers and remained there for several months." After some time Bernadette and the twins were taken to the airport, where she saw the hosting couple receive money from another couple who were buying her babies. In the end both couples were arrested, and the twins were placed in foster care.

The trauma of being raped by her grandfather, beaten by her mother, and becoming pregnant overcame Bernadette. She spent three years in solitary confinement in a mental institution. Steeped in shame, she pledged to herself that she would never discuss her childhood with anyone. It was during this time in the institution that she lost her memory.

In her forties Bernadette began having nightmares and started sleepwalking. She feared burdening others, so these occurrences, too, became her secret.

The breakthrough came when Annette, a friend, visited her before Easter. Bernadette invited her to help make Easter-egg cakes. "I told her we would make sixty cakes to distribute to friends, but I couldn't stop, and continued until I had made three hundred and began loading them into the freezer."

Annette recognized the minibreakdown and called a priest whom both of them knew. This priest invited Bernadette for a visit, and gradually, in disjointed gasps, her story unfolded. When her confidant was eventually transferred, Bernadette became desperate.

"I knew I couldn't go on alone anymore. The nightmares and sleepwalking were so overwhelming, I felt that my promise to hide my secrets no longer counted. I took it upon myself to see a psychologist. Since my priest friend was transferred not too far away, I began visiting him also."

Because the nightmares continue, Bernadette recognizes that it will take some time until she can make sense of what she is remembering. But she is achieving a measure of serenity.

When her mother became ill, Bernadette took her into her home. Hearing impaired and in poor health, without Bernadette's care her mother would have been totally alone. Despite the horrors that her mother inflicted on her, Bernadette cared for her for ten years. When she died in the grip of Alzheimer's disease, she had never expressed remorse for her treatment of Bernadette.

Eventually Bernadette married and adopted a son. Life settled down, and then erupted with new crises—a series of surgeries and hospital stays—six in one year: removal of a mass on her breast, bleeding that could not be controlled, dehydration, inability to keep food down. Week after week, one physical problem after another kept her reeling.

At one point Bernadette was sure that she was dying, so she reviewed her will and made funeral arrangements. She began having violent headaches and pain in her ear and mouth. Her husband urged her to revisit her dentist, who found an infection in her mouth, which took her to the hospital again. Her blood stream had been poisoned from two decayed teeth and the mixture of medicines she was taking. The doctors wanted to know if she was drugging herself into suicide. "No," she replied, "just trying to kill the pain."

Bernadette was given the anointing of the sick twice because she was so close to death. Two weeks before an experimental surgery to which Bernadette had consented, she began bleeding profusely again. "The surgeon had warned me the surgery was experimental, and he could not assure me it would be successful. By this time I was so exhausted from my past surgeries, it didn't really matter what might happen. It took me an hour and a half to come out of the anesthesia. The surgeon didn't leave my side until I was awake. I was happy it was finished."

After this surgery Bernadette was on her feet for the first time in months. By the Christmas holidays, she was roller skating. "I am grateful for the patience and expertise of all the doctors who worked at healing me. It was difficult to have one surgery after another without my body having the opportunity to recuperate. I now understand very concretely the importance of a healthy mind and body. Even though I am still struggling with nightmares and sleepwalking, things are becoming clearer. The support I am receiving from my psychologist and my spiritual director-counselor will help me unravel all my secrets."

They grew gradually, these walls, never quite intentionally.
Before I knew it,
they towered high above me,
suffocating.
Strong they were, mortared with my fear,
forming a dungeon
to claim me as their prisoner.

And then you were there,
straining to bend down
to grasp my fingertips.
You would not let me be.
My heart screamed:
"Leave me alone!
I need to lick my wounds,
to enjoy the pity that I claim!"

But your ears were deaf.
Understanding, encouragement dripped
drop by drop
to melt my resistance.
In your love
you almost leaned too hard.
There was a moment when I felt
you'd be companion in my depths.

But instead you gripped my heart,
pulled, tugged,

encouraged me to scramble,
and, lo, I stood beside you,
looking down into the depths
that would have sucked me under,
buried me in their rubble,
except for your compassion.
Thank you, my friend,
I could not have survived without you.

A back problem began an adventure for Pam that has given her an entirely new perspective on life. The back pain led her to yoga, which has given her relaxation, strength, and flexibility, relieving her of pain.

Her irresistible call to the healing benefits of yoga started slowly. Friends invited her and her aching back to a yoga class. "Once a week we relaxed from toe to head, filled our lungs to bursting with air, and practiced physical postures. I learned there was no competition in yoga, and was inspired to operate in my own circle of perfection, at my own speed, cooperating with the only body I will ever have."

Born in India thousands of years ago, yoga developed to unite the individual with the Absolute Good through meditation, relaxation, and simple body postures. When Pam began practicing yoga three or more times a week, she found that her mood was elevated and she had more energy. "Best of all, I haven't had a muscle spasm in years." Her commitment to yoga has brought her strength, enthusiasm, joy, and energy.

"I do not believe God wants me to mope around with a sore back or rush about feeling irritable and overwhelmed. Yoga helps me feel relaxed and focuses me so I can be a useful instrument for God."

Because yoga was so helpful to her and because there were no yoga teachers in her community, Pam decided to go into training herself. She spent a month at the Sivananda Ashram Yoga Farm in Grass Valley, California. There she made friends with people from France, China, India, New Zealand, Australia, and Argentina. There was time for meditation, yoga philosophy, and four hours of yoga postures daily. A large picture of Jesus painted on the wall of the meditation hall captivated Pam during her reflection time.

She returned as a certified hatha yoga instructor, and now owns White Light Yoga, where she holds classes several times a week. She also joined with two friends in publishing a bimonthly newspaper, the *Turtle River Press*, whose goal is to provide a medium for people to examine a variety of experiences. "We are exploring some of the spiritual expressions happening across the United States. We expect people to read discriminately and to discard what does not fit within their religious culture. The love of Jesus is big enough to embrace and bless everyone, not just those who approach and follow him in a certain way. We're after compassion and peace."

The title was chosen deliberately because of its symbolism. The turtle is a long-standing earth symbol signifying stability, protection, and steady movement. The energy of the turtle's two homes, earth and water, is a reminder that there are times to surrender to the current and times to stand one's ground. The turtle is a dependable teacher, warning of the dangers of pushing the river, of trying to force things. "The turtle can withdraw when fearful or threatened, for he can pull in his head at any time," says Pam. "This is true of our readers. They are free to read whatever they choose and to withdraw from the rest. However, by reading the newspaper, they become acquainted with other expressions of spirituality."

River represents the flow of energy, spirit, and insight that are present within the pages. The river flows through time, connecting people to what was and what is to come. It also symbolizes life, strength, healing, and cleansing. The home of the *Turtle River Press* is located where two rivers converge, creating a powerful stream of energy. This publication of creative energy has found its roots here where the rivers meet, intensifying the flow of life.

Healing doesn't just happen.
It needs an invitation, an inner, expectant climate.
Healing invites the Creator
to create us whole again.

Cleveland, Ohio, and Klaipeda, Lithuania, are sister cities bonded together because of the needs of Klaipeda and the resources of Cleveland. Their partnership is more than an agreement on paper. This is evident in the medical help Cleveland's doctors and nurses have given to facially deformed youngsters in Klaipeda.

Dr. Gintautas Sabataitis, a clinical psychologist who speaks English, Lithuanian, French, and German, is the director of the nonprofit Partnership in Hope program begun in 1995. Through his organizational efforts, medical teams are recruited for mercy missions to the central European country.

When Lithuania was under the domination of Russia, communism stifled the economy and limited contact with the West. Medical equipment and care were primitive. The families of sick people had to buy syringes and medicine for the ones who were ill.

Dr. John DiStafano, clinical professor at Case Western Reserve University (CWRU), and Dr. Jerold Goldberg, chairman of oral-maxillofacial surgery and dean of CWRU, had gone on a mercy mission to Lithuania in 1992 to perform reconstructive facial surgery. The great needs impressed both doctors, and they decided to return to Lithuania. To support their efforts and to recruit other medical personnel, Grace Kudikis and Dr. Sabataitis organized Partnership in Hope as a nonprofit organization.

Dr. Sabataitis and all the physicians sought donations from health-care companies, vendors, hospitals, social-service groups, and company representatives. Individuals were also eager to help. In late May and early June 1995, a thirteen-member team left for Klaipeda. It included the facial surgeons, an anesthesiologist, pediatricians, orthodontists, a pediatric dentist, a family dentist, and two operating-room nurses. They operated pro bono. Fourteen children were helped by this visit.

Dr. DiStafano acknowledged: "The Lithuanian doctors have surgical skills, but not the needed equipment to perform the operations efficiently. Suspecting that, we brought foot lockers full of medical supplies, including an anesthesia machine, and left everything in Klaipeda." The doctors evaluated thirty-six other children for future medical help. They also taught the repair techniques to Lithuanian surgeons, and Dr.

Vytautas Griksas, a staff neurosurgeon at the hospital in Klaipeda, came to Cleveland University Hospital as a trainee.

The team returned in May 1996, and again in May 1997. It was during this latter visit that the Klaipeda hospital dedicated a new oral and maxillofacial surgery unit as the DiStafano and Goldberg Center. During this visit the team performed twenty-two surgeries as they trained additional doctors.

Dr. Sabataitis tells the story of Tomas, a seventeen-year-old boy who was born without a lower jaw and chin. "His upper jaw receded and was slanted to the left. Tomas was in constant pain and had trouble speaking, eating, and smiling. He was so disfigured, people would turn away in horror when they saw him. The doctors in Lithuania did not have the skills or the medical equipment needed for such a surgery. Drs. DiStafano and Goldberg agreed to operate on Tomas if he would come to Cleveland.

"Paule Balciunas, age ninety-three, read an article about Tomas and began collecting money at the senior center where she lived. In spite of the poverty of the residents, she was able to collect three thousand dollars for airfare for Tomas, his mother, and two doctors who needed to learn what to do in follow-up surgeries. Sadly, Paule died five months before Tomas came to Cleveland."

In surgery the doctors took a bone from Tomas's hip and made another jaw. They also straightened his upper jawbone and brought it forward. Dr. John Michael Smith, a pediatric dentist in Parma Heights, Ohio, prepared braces and fillings for Tomas. Tomas went home with a smile on his face that does not cause pain. Dr. Sabataitis rejoices, "He no longer fears the ridicule that was heaped upon him before."

The trips to Lithuania continue. In 1998 fifteen visiting doctors performed nineteen surgeries in five days. They brought operating tables, anesthesia machines, Eagle monitors to monitor vital signs, and medications, and they equipped two operating rooms with lights. The doctors they trained had completed four hundred fifty surgeries in one year. Now Case Western Reserve and Klaipeda Hospitals are connected via satellite for teleconferencing about cases.

Dr. Sabataitis has strong motivation for carrying on this mission, because he is not a stranger to pain. As a young boy, his family escaped Lithuania to East Prussia when the Russians occupied the country. On the run, the family moved from one location to another until they finally arrived at a refugee camp set up by the United Nations Relief Organization in Wiesbaden, Germany. They spent two years in the camp. The Immigration Act of 1948 allowed refugees to enter the United States, so the family moved once again, landing at Ellis Island. Sponsored by relatives in Chicago, the Sabataitis family took the first train they could get to the Midwest.

After finishing high school in Chicago, Gintautas entered the Jesuits and was ordained a priest. He taught in high schools, hospitals, and universities, was chaplain for the 8th Infantry Division, and an assistant editor of a Lithuanian publication. Some years after departing the Jesuits, he married Camille.

When Gintautas received his doctorate in clinical psychology from Case Western Reserve University, he began his practice in Parma, Ohio, a suburb of Cleveland. "There are many Lithuanians in this area," says Dr. Sabataitis. "It was they who decided they wanted a sister city in Lithuania after the country won its independence. When the Lithuanians discovered what Drs. DiStafano and Goldberg had done on their mercy missions, they wanted the mission to become an annual event.

"Although the team pays for its trip and other expenses, my task is to raise funds for medicines and equipment. Rotary International has been especially helpful. It has equipped two operating rooms and is planning to equip a surgical intensive-care unit. Finnair gives us travel discounts as well as luggage allowances to transport the heavy equipment we take with us. We also have many individual donors. Because of all this help, we have confidence this project will continue until Lithuanian doctors have learned the skills and gained the expertise to do it on their own."

All of us need healing,
some of us more than others.
Physical disabilities
can make life seem merciless.
Hope and solace come
when the compassionate and the caring
offer their love through skill and talent, and selfless sacrifice,
promoting a time of healing.

TIME FOR FORGIVING

When we have been hurt, we suffer. If the pain simmers, it gnaws at our mind, causing our heart to harden. Sometimes we are justly accused, but to protect ourselves we simply deny or ignore the accusation. At times we are blameless, but we still can suffer a lost reputation and a broken spirit that may fill us with hatred and a desire for revenge.

The urge to retaliate can become a millstone dragging us into unknown darkness within ourselves. Each time the memory of the wrong returns, it fans the embers of our hatred or resentment. Allowed to continue, this anger can turn to rage, which in turn can lead to disastrous consequences and fractured relationships.

We can turn to the forgiving Christ hanging on his tree. Then we may begin to let go of those memories that disrupt our life, move forward to regain a measure of peace. Eventually we can say the Lord's Prayer with sincerity, for we too have need of forgiveness.

Letting go of disruptive memories does not ensure they will be eradicated. But such memories need not control our life. By praying for the persons who have hurt us, we also do ourselves a favor. We heal our emotions gradually. With God's grace we come to a time to forgive. If we accept the blessing, we accept the gifts that come from forgiveness.

Her husband didn't want a divorce, but he didn't want to give up his girlfriend either. Gloria had been married to him for twenty years, and they had three teenage children. He had started coming home late and was not himself. She confronted her husband, who admitted he was having an affair.

Gloria knew that he could not live with the family, and she insisted he move out. The children were devastated when they were told.

He did move out, but only for short periods of time. Each time he left, his conscience bothered him, and he would return. He did not want to leave his family and all the things he had worked for over the years. He seemed to be under a spell.

"Throughout this traumatic time, I knew I loved him," Gloria says. "I worked to keep my mind off the situation and pleaded with God for a change on his part. I wanted my life and our marriage back." Because the children saw how painful the situation was for their mother, they did not want their father to return.

Suddenly a blood clot threw his lover into a coma. She died within a week. He stayed separated from the family for almost a year after her death, but he visited them frequently and seemed genuinely sorry.

Two more years passed before Gloria's husband returned permanently, repentant and grateful the family could forgive. "Our life has returned to normal," Gloria notes, "but I know things will never be quite the same. I thank God daily that we were able to reclaim, at least partially, that which we had lost."

Even though others had encouraged Gloria not to take him back, she trusted circumstances would change and is satisfied with the way things have straightened out. He has tried to make amends for bringing this sorrow to his family.

"I am glad I did not listen to the advice others offered me. The two years brought much sorrow and distress and have taught me a great deal. I have learned not to take life for granted, for things can change unexpectedly. I am also convinced that when I put my trust in God, God will not let me down. I have forgiven my husband, and I am at peace."

To forgive—
this slow process of transforming hatred into love
frees us from the prison of resentment,
enabling us to continue with life.
Forgiveness heals our enemy
as well as ourselves.

Watching the Gestapo gun down her father in a wheat field is a scene burned into Aldona's memory. Soon afterward the Nazis stormed into her house and took her away from her three-year-old sister and five-year-old brother. She never saw them again. The Nazis later killed her mother, two other brothers, and a twin sister.

When she could no longer endure prison, Aldona escaped. The SS soldiers were executing some prisoners when she crawled through a barbed-wire fence, having burrowed a small tunnel with her bare hands and slid through it, badly injuring her back.

Bleeding painfully, Aldona ran into the forest. She found a sewer pipe and crawled through it. When she emerged she saw two German women picking mushrooms and berries. These blood sisters sheltered her in their home. She was twelve years old. During the thirteen years Aldona lived with the women, she spoke German, forgetting her native Lithuanian language.

When Aldona was six years old, she had made a promise to the Virgin Mary that she would become a nun. At that time her chances for this happening were slim because the family was too poor to educate her. However, after thirteen years in Germany, she had gotten an education and was earning her own living. The dream simmered in Aldona. "I can now keep my promise to the Virgin," she thought. "I can enter the convent to make amends for the Nazis and the Communists who ravaged my homeland and killed my family. I have forgiven them, but in the convent I can pray and do reparation for them."

A Lithuanian Capuchin priest advised her to enter a Lithuanian community, and since her homeland was still under Communist rule, she could not risk returning to it. So in 1957 she applied to the Sisters of Saint Casimir, a Lithuanian community in Chicago. Her religious name became Sister Mary Zita. "When Lithuania and the other Baltics regained their independence from the Soviets in 1990, I rejoiced."

Forty years after Aldona had entered the United States—now a U.S. citizen—she returned to visit her homeland. She found cousins, and she discovered that one of her sisters whom she had thought was dead had survived both the Gestapo and the Communists. She now believes that this sister died in the Chernobyl accident.

Sister Mary Zita has forgiven: "I pray continuously for Lithuania, asking God to restore and strengthen her religious and historic heritage. Even though I am now far away from my land of birth, Lithuania remains a memory deep in my heart. But divine providence has led me to the United States, and I am making it my home and my mission."

Forgiveness takes a decision—
to let go of retaliation,
to seek the transformation of our pain.
Wounds persist,
but God grants grace to change the past
through a spiritual surgery of hatred
that absolves the transgressor
and gently subdues the ache.

Two years ago I was invited to lead an interdenominational conference for missionaries in Thailand. Sponsored by an ad hoc committee, it was the first time the various Protestant and Evangelical missionaries had ever been together with Roman Catholic priests and nuns for a teaching retreat. The first day was tense as some of the Evangelicals were forced to interface with Roman Catholics. However, by the end of the second day, the atmosphere had cleared, and it seemed the groups were actually going to be able to flow together in some kind of unity.

The final afternoon, in a meeting in a large, screened pavilion overlooking the Gulf, I spoke on forgiveness. At the close of my teaching session, even before I left the speaker's stand, a Roman Catholic nun stepped forward from the group. She was French, and had been a missionary to the Thai people for a number of years. She knelt before me and crossed herself.

"For many years I have held deep grudges against the Protestants who came into Thailand and built on the foundations laid by the Catholic church. I have been highly critical, and I need forgiveness. Will you pray for me?"

I started to respond, for it was the very subject I had been teaching. But as I stepped forward to pray for her, I felt checked. I stepped back and heard myself saying, "No, Sister, I am not the one to pray for you. You have made your confession and now you are absolved from your sin. I want to ask those here who have felt resentment or bitterness toward you to come and pray for you. In so doing they will receive forgiveness themselves."

I stepped to one side and left her kneeling on the concrete floor. At once several people got to their feet and came forward. Then several others. In all almost a dozen men and women stood around the kneeling nun. It was a touching moment. There were few dry eyes in the room.

When the prayer was over, those who had prayed for the Catholic sister embraced her and started back for their seats. I stepped forward to close the meeting with a prayer when a man in the front row stood up and spoke out.

"Before we leave I have something I want to say. I have been in Thailand for eight years. During that time I felt our group was the only spiritual people in the nation. Like Sister Rene I have been highly critical of others, not only of the Catholics but also of the Pentecostals. I have been wrong. I ask forgiveness of all of you."

His voice was choking as he sat down. Immediately three other people were on their feet, all trying to speak at once, all confessing their bad attitudes and critical natures, asking forgiveness. They finally slowed down long enough to take turns, but by the time they had finished, others were standing. I stepped back to one side and let the meeting carry itself.

After about forty-five minutes, it seemed we were finished. I stepped up to the front once again to close the meeting. When I did, one other man in the back row stood up. His face was hard, his lips white with anger.

"I have been sitting here for almost an hour," he said, "while all this garbage has been going on. I have tried as hard as I could to keep my mouth shut. But I must speak. My father was an Evangelical missionary in Colombia, South America. I was raised on the mission field. I can remember, as an eight-year-old boy, hiding with my parents behind a clump of bushes while a mob of Roman Catholics, led by the local priest, brought torches and set fire to the little church building my father had built with his own hands.

"The next year I was with my father in the mountains of Colombia. We were visiting an old man who was dying of tuberculosis. Just three weeks before, he had accepted Christ as his Savior, and he allowed my father to pray with him. That afternoon, after we had walked three hours to reach his little hut, we were sitting beside his bed and my father was reading the Bible to him.

"Suddenly the Roman Catholic priest burst into the hut. 'If you do not renounce this false religion,' he said sternly, 'you will be excommunicated from the church and denied entrance into heaven when you die.' I was too frightened to remain, and ran from the hut in tears. My father stayed to argue, but was told he should leave if he valued his life. He was told he had no business interfering with the affairs of the church."

The man stopped speaking and looked around the room. A few heads had turned and were now looking at him. "That is the reason I cannot tolerate what has been taking place here this afternoon," he said. "If you had been hurt by Roman Catholics as deeply as I have, you would understand."

There was not a sound. He stood, physically shaking, trying to recover his composure enough to sit down. Before he could, however, one of the old Catholic priests in the front row stood up. He turned to the man and began to speak, slowly but deliberately.

"My son, many years ago I was just out of school and went as a missionary to Colombia. It is very possible I was there when you were there, for I am now an old man and you are still young. It matters not, for at that time I had been trained to believe all Evangelicals and Protestants were heretics. I do not know if I was the one who came into that old man's house, but it very well could have been me, for I did many things like that."

He paused and looked around the group. Every eye was on him as he spoke. "But many changes have taken place since then. Now we see you not as our enemies but as our brothers. And not only has there been a change in the church but there has been a change in me. Now I ask you, my son, to forgive. Forgive the Roman Catholic church. Forgive me."

He pushed aside his chair and started back toward where the missionary was standing. But before he had gone through one row of chairs, the man came rushing to meet him, shoving aside chairs to grab him in a tight, tearful embrace. The other people in the group came rushing toward them to form a huge knot in the middle of the room, a mass of loving, forgiving, weeping, laughing believers. (This story comes from *Coping with Criticism*, by Jamie Buckingham, and is used with permission.)

The power of the Holy Spirit
is full of possibility.
Even in unimaginable situations,
the Spirit gathers courage,
purges the festering infection of hate,
resurrects into wholeness
the demolished fragments of relationships.

TIME FOR JUSTICE

In doing justice we shall behold the face of God (cf. Psalm 17:15), and in God's time there is always time for justice. Indeed, God rewards us according to our justice (cf. Psalm 18:21). Yet hatred and fear frequently gnaw away our resolve to mete out justice to others as we would want justice for ourselves. We strike out overtly and covertly, and when we do, we diminish the honor not only of the one we have harmed but also of ourselves. Our actions are like throwing stones at our own glass house.

We are unjust in numerous ways. We ignore others because they are poor or unlikable, because they threaten us for some reason, because we are blind and deaf to their needs, because doing justice might require more effort on our part than we are willing to give.

Redemption lies in acknowledging that we are all God's children, created in God's image and likeness. We need to accept our brothers and sisters, no matter who or where they might be, unless we are looking for the same kind of retribution.

The tattooed number B11291 on the inside of his left arm is a constant reminder to Henry Oertelt of the horrors of being a Jew during the reign of Hitler. So are the scars on his body and the memories of the dehumanization the Germans perpetrated.

When Hitler came to power in 1933, he built his first concentration camp in Dachau, near Munich, for political prisoners. Other camps sprang up, and systematic murdering began. Hitler ordered a boycott of all Jewish establishments. The Gestapo forced Jews to wear the infamous six-pointed star on a yellow background with the word Jew boldly inscribed in the center. Henry still has this insignia.

Born in and a citizen of Germany, Henry did not accept the status of a second-class citizen. He was not about to surrender his right to walk the streets freely, to visit movie theaters, restaurants, concert halls, or other public places. He designed his own star out of tin, glued material over it, soldered a pin on its back and stuck the insignia on his jacket whenever he left home. As soon as the streets were clear, he would take it off and put it in his pocket. Thus he had free movement and ignored the curfew.

The Nazis enslaved Henry and other Jews to do menial jobs. Like horses they had to pull wagons full of rock and dirt. They received ration cards, but got only half the rations. Sometimes the card would be snipped in half so rations could be cut some more. School children would come to the workplace on buses to view the motley-looking crew of workers as they were building roads with primitive implements. Egged on by their teachers, the children ridiculed the Jewish workers.

By 1938 Henry and all other Jews had totally lost their freedom, citizenship, and jobs. When a Jew killed a German government official in Paris, Kristallnacht exploded. Jewish-owned apartments, houses, and synagogues in Germany and Austria were destroyed, and the Holocaust began. Thirty thousand wealthy Jews were rounded up and sent to concentration camps. Some who could pay the demanded extortion had twenty-four hours to leave the country.

On 1 September 1939, Hitler marched into Poland, and as he conquered Austria, France, Belgium, the Baltics, Czechoslovakia, Holland, and Hungary, he constructed additional extermination camps. For two more years, Henry did street work in Berlin.

In 1941 Hitler ran out of skilled workers, so Jews with special skills were given unexpected opportunities. Henry was one of the fortunate ones. He began working in a furniture factory. As a boy he had been apprenticed to a Christian who taught him woodworking and furniture building.

Then in May 1943, the inevitable happened to Henry's family. At 2:00 a.m. the Gestapo appeared at their door, gave them fifteen minutes to pack one suitcase apiece, and took them to the railroad station. The train brought them to the German concentration camp in Terezin, Czechoslovakia. Henry's mother, his brother Kurt, and Kurt's fiance, Sonja, were all on the same train. Upon arrival, his mother and Sonja were sent to the women's part of the camp, but Henry and Kurt stayed together.

In October 1944, because space was needed for incoming prisoners, many of those in Terezin were moved again, this time packed into cattle cars without food, water, or toilet facilities. At the end of two harrowing days, they arrived at the gates of Auschwitz, Poland. Here the children, the sick, and the old were separated out. Because they were useless as workers, they were sent to the gas chambers.

After Henry and the other men showered, all their body hair was shorn. They were given prisoners' clothes. Forbidden to use their own names, numbers were tattooed on their left arms. When they lined up before work and were asked their name, they were kicked in the stomach or the groin if they gave it. If they forgot the number and looked at their arm, they were immediately brutalized.

The prisoners, men and women, worked ten to twelve hours daily. At times they were lined up to watch men beaten to death and hung. Frequently an SS guard would challenge a man to run. Of course he would be shot when he ran, or shot if he did not obey.

Because the Russians were closing in and pushing the SS toward Bavaria, after four months in Auschwitz, Henry, Kurt, and Sonja were moved to the concentration camp in Flossenburg, the same camp where Bonhoeffer, the German theologian, was killed. Henry's mother was no longer with them. She had been sent to the gas chamber in Auschwitz.

In Flossenburg Henry faced a dilemma. He had developed an infection, a swelling the size of an orange, under his left arm. Kurt had been sent outside the camp to work. Knowing how ill Henry was, he felt helpless to support him. Henry knew that his survival was in jeopardy, for all sick prisoners incapable of work were murdered.

Going to a Flossenburg SS doctor was perilous. These doctors would check those who came for medical help, but if they showed any weakness, the surgeons would cut open their swellings without anesthesia. They were then sent to the sick barracks to await the gas chamber. So when Henry appeared before the surgeon, he stood up straight as he described his swelling in short, military words. The SS officer attending him was impressed by his courage, and gave him anesthesia before lancing the swelling. He sent Henry to the sick barracks, but each time the general came through, he overlooked Henry.

Henry was grateful, but he had seen the officer beating and kicking sick prisoners before sending them to the "convalescent home" for destruction. Indeed, there were enough witnesses to this man's cruelty during the Nuremberg Trials in 1945 to execute him.

From Flossenburg the prisoners were sent on a death march, for General Patton and his troops were moving into Germany. The prisoners marched for two days, and anyone who collapsed was immediately shot, put into a truck, and taken to a mass grave. During this march, and at the end of his strength, Henry saw an armored column flying the American flag. When he was liberated, Henry weighed eighty-two pounds. After he regained sufficient strength, he started his seven-hundred-mile walk back to Berlin. He and Kurt had agreed to return there if they survived. At times military vehicles would give him a ride.

Kurt, however, was convinced that Henry had died in Flossenburg because he had been so ill. So Kurt went to Munich instead. Henry, along with other returnees, put up notices asking for information about missing relatives. A man told Henry that he had seen his brother in Munich. The connection was soon made.

Eventually Henry married Inge, whom he had known before the war. In 1949, when they received displaced-persons' status, they emigrated to the United States. Kurt, however, was unable to leave with his brother. He had married Sonja while in the camps, but she had contracted tuberculosis. Kurt had to wait for her to heal. By 1951 both Henry and Kurt had found their haven in the United States.

Today Henry Oertelt lives in Saint Paul, Minnesota. "I have dedicated my life to telling the story of the Holocaust so no one would ever doubt it happened." His memories of the horrors will always remain with him, but his spirit is healed. He is convinced his story will remain a part of Jewish history, and that keeping the story alive may help prevent this kind of horrible injustice from happening again.

Inhumanity!
When hatred, greed, vengeance
lay claim to minds, hearts, and spirits,
there is no impartiality or justice.
There is only violation, torture, murder.
Injustice is rampant.

All of us are culpable.
Divine and human laws are disregarded
by those who seek to make gods of themselves,
destroying the foundation of what it means to be human.

I am a Palestinian," says George, "but I cannot admit my identity when I am in Israel. When an Israeli soldier asks me who
I am, I must answer I am an Arab or a Christian or a Muslim, but never a Palestinian. Sanctions follow if I claim my real identity."

George's home in Jerusalem is in the wall of the Old City near
the Muslim Gate. He can look out of the slits and see the people in the
street. It was here he and his siblings were born, giving them the right
to Israeli citizenship. But they can never claim these rights for themselves. They must carry special identity cards and present them whenever they are asked for them.

The license plates on their cars identify not only their personal
identity but also the place where they live. Cars are constantly stopped
and searched. George and Palestinians like him are arrested upon sus-
picion and put into prison without trial. His mother was hit by soldiers. A brother was beaten. Two brothers were jailed for four months
without trial.

"Because the military makes it clear they are in control through
their tactics, they do everything to make us feel hopeless. Our social
and cultural events are always monitored. If we apply for permits of
any kind, these are delayed for months."

Today George lives in the United States, but his memories of
abuse remain vivid. He recalls the pain and frustration he felt when his
mother needed a kidney transplant. The military doctor made no effort
to help her. Eventually she received a permit to go to Iraq, where she
got her transplant. When she died in November 1994, George's permit
was delayed three weeks, so he was unable to return for her funeral.
An American friend visiting Israel a year later was able to bring back a
photo of his mother's grave.

"I felt so hopeless, recognizing there was no future even if I
earned a degree at a Palestinian university. Palestinians are not allowed

to compete economically, so I got a permit to study in the United States instead."

He lost his right to Israeli residency because he was out of the country for three years. "Where can we students get money to fly back to Israel every three years? Having earned degrees in politics, administration, biological and computer sciences, and law, Palestinians could liberate their people from enslavement. This is why Israelis restrain educated people from returning. Why does the Israeli government always find multiple reasons to sabotage the peace process?"

George had not yet been born when the oppression of the Palestinians began in 1948, but he knows his history. "Hundreds of our villages were bulldozed or confiscated. We estimate about two-hundred-billion-dollars' worth of property was taken away from us. I know this confiscation is still going on because my family's land on the West Bank was taken away. It had been handed down through generations, but we had no document to prove it was ours.

"The Israelis build their settlements on Palestinian land that they have taken from our people, and we are supposed to take it meekly. But when an Israeli Palestinian, in October 1997, attempted to live in Jerusalem near Mea Shearim, her home was firebombed and she was forced to move."

Israeli Palestinians make up about one million of Israel's 5.9 million people. Most speak Hebrew as well as Arabic and pay taxes, but their rights are drastically curtailed. Israelis fear the growth of Palestinian families, for these can easily outnumber their own.

"I doubt I would be alive today if I had not left Israel. All I saw was injustice and hatred," says George. "I could not have stood aside and let it continue. From frustration I left the country to prepare myself to return someday, ready to help my people."

George came to the United States when he was nineteen. Since then he has earned a degree in electronic engineering and has had experience in technical and manufacturing jobs. He is adept in computer programming. He knows these skills will be helpful when he returns. This education and experience would not have been his if he had opted to study in Israel. Palestinian universities are closed for the slightest reasons, sometimes for as long as a year. Those who want to complete their course work attend underground classes that move from location to location during the shutdowns. When they graduate they can find only menial jobs.

Happily married with three children, George is an American citizen. Yet his heart rests in Palestine. He has removed himself from hateful and unjust behavior. He does not want to become like the enemy. "The enemy dictates behavior. If the enemy is ruthless and violent, then it invites the same in return."

Instead George dreams. Someday he will return to Palestine to set up youth centers to provide opportunities for the next generation to live with dignity and hope. "I have had mentors here who have helped me. I hope to provide that kind of mentoring for my own people.

"I want to tell my story, for the pen is mightier than the sword. I wonder if people in the States are aware of the bondage under which Palestinians live. Do Americans know that fourteen million dollars a day of taxpayer money goes to Israel, a nation that routinely violates the moral and legal principles of the United States and its Constitution? They call us terrorists when we fight for our rights. But decades ago, when they used terroristic techniques to remove us from our land and to bomb the King David Hotel in Jerusalem, the Jews considered that patriotism.

"In a sense I feel they are doing to us what the Gestapo did to them in World War II. It may not be as dramatically visible, but its subtlety is just as effective. We are half brothers fathered by Abraham. Why can't we live together in peace? Will hatred always be a wedge between us?"

Justice is a conundrum
sealed within our perceptions.
The enigma lies in the way we discern
our rights as opposed to those of others.
Hatred, first from one side and then the other,
incites retaliation that knows no termination.
An eye for an eye makes humanity blind.
(Ghandi)

Bud Welch never tires of talking about his daughter Julie. On 19 April 1995, she died in the bombing of the Murrah Building in Oklahoma City. She had been to Mass that morning, and two hours after receiving the Eucharist, she was welcomed home by God. She was only twenty-three years old.

Julie had been a foreign exchange student in Spain between her sophomore and junior high school years. In college she spent her sophomore year in Madrid at Marquette University's institution there. By the time she received her degree, she was fluent in Spanish, Italian, French, Portuguese, and German. She was working as a Spanish translator in the social security office when she was killed.

The parking lot across the street is special for Bud. A diseased elm tree that had broken through the asphalt eighty years ago and was filled with the mistletoe parasite was a favorite spot for Julie. She would park her car in its shade each morning. Bud visits it, leans against it, closes his eyes, listens to the leaves, and thinks about the way it used to be when they would meet for lunch at a Greek restaurant across from the Murrah Building every Wednesday.

The ancient elm is the only living thing left in the area, even though the leaves were torn off by the bombing. It is now called the Survivor Tree. The city took seedlings from it, and on the second anniversary of the bombing, handed out fourteen-inch offspring to survivors. To ensure the tree's survival, four branches were also planted, with the hope that these clones would become permanent reminders of the tragedy.

The block where the building stood has been closed since the bombing and will never be reopened. Bud served on the committee to plan the memorial that stands where the building once did. At the dedication, Vice President Gore declared, "Today we gather to seek the light, to find in this soil, nourished with a million tears, the harvest of God's healing grace." Now no one will forget the tragedy that struck Oklahoma City.

Two years after the disaster, Bud received a letter from Stacey, a young woman who had been at Marquette when Julie was studying there. She hadn't known Julie too well, but Julie's death had had a profound effect. She told Bud that she had attended the memorial service on the campus, for she needed some personal comfort, and she told him of the following event.

About a week after the service, as Stacey was driving home on a weekday evening, She was busy concentrating on work at the office and the slow-moving traffic. Julie had not entered her thoughts until the moment she looked up and saw an amazing sunset. "The sunshine sort of wrapped itself around the clouds," she wrote. "Light streamed in through the billowy puffs in an array of bright yellow colors I have never seen before or since. This sounds corny, and I don't know how religious your family is, but it was almost as if heaven were leaking through the clouds. It was truly spectacular.

"I can't explain why, but my immediate and uncontrollable reaction was to giggle. I was laughing, and I actually said out loud, 'Hey, Julie.' For that moment I felt happy, content, and almost giddy, because I knew that Julie, through that beautiful sunset, had said 'Hello' first."

Bud struggles with his mixed feelings about Timothy McVeigh. He wants McVeigh punished, but he is unsure whether he wants him dead. He remembers a conversation with Julie when they were driving to Milwaukee one year. During a radio talk show, a reporter was discussing the execution that had taken place that day in Texas. Julie had exclaimed: "How terrible. There's no redeeming social value in killing. It only fosters hate."

Bud also reflects on two calls he received, one from Texas and the other from Florida. The callers expressed the guilt and depression they felt because of the executions. "You don't need this guilt in your life," one of them said. "Don't fall prey to vengeance and hate." These cautions haunt Bud, and he wonders what good it will do to have McVeigh executed.

Bud attended the last week of the trial in Denver. He could see no remorse, no regret for the murders. "If only McVeigh would have shown some sorrow, I would find it easier to forgive. Killing him will not bring Julie or any of the others back. Jesus has asked us to forgive our enemies. I don't know if I am up to that at present."

Bud also hopes that if McVeigh is not executed, he just might talk. "If he's in prison long enough, McVeigh may tell us what his thought processes were, why he did what he did, and who else was involved. I want to hear that information, even if it comes out as bragging.

"Julie was my pal, my confidant. That Survivor Tree always speaks to me when I stop there after Sunday Mass. I see Julie in her little red Grand Am, parked in the shade. As we talk things over, I feel at peace." Julie's Aunt Gerarda wrote the following poem to commemorate the Survivor Tree. Regardless of what other memorials emerge, this tree will have been the only witness to the catastrophe.

A loud boom and shrill,
     hurtling, flying debris;
     smoke's in my face.
I can't see anything.

My limbs have fallen,
     they're twisted and torn.
I'm shocked and bewildered
     at the injustice and ruin.

People running to help
     in the building 'round here:
     commotion, sirens, panic,
     unbelievable terror and fear.

I wish I could assist
     this catastrophe to erase.
I'm shocked and bewildered
     at the injustice and ruin.

I remember that morning,
     my friends were happy, alive.
Now they are injured.
     I pray they will survive.

Days, nights have gone by;
     special doctors comfort me.
I hear one of them say,
     "You are now the 'Survivor Tree.'"

As time makes its journey,
     nature's work is profound
     to repair and to heal me,
     grow grass in Sacred Ground.

Soon construction will begin
    to beautify these grounds.
Strength I will need to endure
    the hammering, clanking sounds.

I wonder what could be more lovely
    than the grass, the fence, and me,
    and the many offerings of love
    placed here by passersby.

It's autumn and I am tired;
    the Master expects much of me.
Before my friends were born,
    I was a young, vibrant tree.

So much healing has to be done;
    these people depend on me.
I promise to devote myself
    to inherited tasks and duty.

No matter what it takes,
    I'll be here to lift them up
    until their grief disappears,
    until they are old enough.

My roots are planted here.
I'll neither go nor cease
    until the people who need me
    are reborn to a "Divine Grace."

Bud and his wife, upon invitation, attended a meeting of the National Association of Criminal Defense Lawyers in New York City. Six hundred attorneys were present. Bud was given the Champion of Justice Award, and in his acceptance speech, he remarked, "On the heels of the death sentence of Timothy McVeigh, I am not sure all of you understand how difficult it can be to hold a minority opinion on an issue so fraught with emotion as capital punishment.

"I listened with amazement as people talked about how right the death sentence was, how necessary, how appropriate. Even the governor said, 'All Oklahomans can feel proud of the verdict.' I don't, and not because I am soft on crime. If any crime ever deserved the death penalty, this one did.

"The question for me is not just one of deterrence or the necessity of accepting the ultimate penalty for one of the most horrendous crimes in history. The question is whether or not this so-called Christian nation cares to wrestle honestly with the seemingly impossible demands of the Gospels.

"I am not all that interested in what Governor Frank Keating thinks, and you should not be interested in what Bud Welch thinks. But we should all be interested in what Jesus of Nazareth thinks. If we are going to quote the Bible in support of the death penalty, then for heaven's sake, let's not forget there is a New Testament.

"Everytime anyone gives a speech in support of capital punishment, which is a position most Americans take, they never fail to quote this Old Testament passage. But I have never, not even once, heard a single person quote Matthew 5:38–39, otherwise known as the Sermon on the Mount.

"Jesus said, 'You have heard it said an eye for an eye and a tooth for a tooth, but I say to you, if a man strikes you on one cheek, turn also to him the other.' Ghandi put it beautifully, 'An eye for an eye leaves the whole world blind.'

"If you have heard one single thing I said as diminishing by one iota the indescribable pain of that great city in the lower Midwest or of the families of those killed, or the heroism that everyone displayed, then you heard me wrong. I have never been, nor do I hope ever to be again, so close to something so horrible.

"The local and national news media appeared to be in shock that I would state publicly my position on the death penalty."

Trust in God who will act,
bringing forth your vindication as the light.
(Psalm 37:5–6)

You love justice and hate wickedness,
therefore, God, your God, has anointed you.
(Psalm 45:7)

In the path of righteousness there is life,
in walking its path there is no death.
(Proverbs 12:28)

A fire in his soul impels Bill Duna to tell the story of his people. He is a Rom, a Gypsy, as well as a citizen of the United States, whose family of musicians came from Slovakia over a century ago. They played music and made and repaired string instruments.

The history of Bill's immediate family reaches back to his great-grandfather Gega Duna, whose passion was music. In 1905 the family orchestra, renowned for its waltz music, played at the World's Fair in Chicago. Later, after settling in Cleveland, Gega gave music lessons to members of the Cleveland Symphony Orchestra, but was not allowed to play in it simply because he was a Rom.

Bill was born in Cleveland, and eventually the family moved to the north side of Chicago. He left there in 1969 to come to the Twin Cities in Minnesota. The love of music passed down through generations still courses in Bill's heart, and he continues this legacy through Bill Duna Productions, his own band, which can shift from a trio to ten pieces and a varied repertoire. In addition he teaches jazz theory and piano. But his greatest interest is telling the stories of the Romani, whom we know as Gypsies. He has a platform for this at the University of Saint Thomas, where he teaches courses on the history of the Gypsies.

"Gypsies are not well known in this country," says Bill. "We have large extended families, and children get plenty of affirmations, which keeps them out of gangs." What Bill finds refreshing is that children are listened to and have no need to extend their egos. They develop their musical talents because they bring joy to themselves and to others with it.

Bill was appointed to the United States Holocaust Council by President Reagan, and then reappointed by President Bush. He continues to serve on the council, and travels around the world sharing the story of the Holocaust of the Gypsies, which has been kept secret for decades.

The Roma originally migrated from India, and spoke the Sanskrit language that was passed on orally. They are a true Aryan race, and became nomads as they traveled into Europe after the Persian War, around 800 C.E. They became known as Romani or Sinti (the people), and settled in Greece, Russia, Slovakia, Hungary, Romania, Poland, and Spain. They worked as coppersmiths, blacksmiths, horse dealers, violin makers, entertainers, healers, trainers of dancing bears, and fortune tellers. Russia welcomed them for their skill in animal husbandry.

During the plague of the Middle Ages, because the Romani were healers, they were able to cure themselves with herbs and through isolation. Because others could not comprehend why so many people everywhere were dying, but most of the Romanis were not, the Romanis became scapegoats. Persecutions began, and Bill tells of these with vivid detail. The Romani were forced to live on society's fringes. They became nomads or were placed in ghettos. To protect themselves from this rejection, they gathered in numbers, formed their own culture, and maintained as much of their linguistic continuity and identity as possible.

"I am a Catholic," says Bill. "It saddens me to know the Catholic church participated in the persecution of the Romani during the Middle Ages because it felt threatened by the dark people entering Europe from Egypt. These Romani eventually began to be called 'Gypsies,' and the peasants were attracted to them. But they were coming from a Muslim country, and the church felt that Mohammedanism was a menace to Christianity.

"Because the church saw them as a threat, it imprisoned them, sold them for cheap labor, blamed them for whatever catastrophe occurred. Because the Gypsies were so skilled, trade guilds were resentful and passed laws prohibiting them from working."

By the early 1300s, laws made the Gypsies slaves. The Council of Trent (1545–1563) excluded the Gypsy men from the priesthood. In Prussia in 1725, Frederick William I ordered all Gypsies over eighteen to be hanged. That same year Charles VI of the Holy Roman Empire condemned the men to death. Women's right ears were severed in Bohemia; in Silesia and Moravia, it was their left ears. Columbus, on his voyages to the New World, took Gypsy women on his ships as sexual objects for the sailors. The Romani had no country to retreat to. They had no military, political, or economic strength in Western Europe.

To escape persecution in Europe, some Romani carried fraudulent letters of protection from the pope and from Sigmund, emperor of the Holy Roman Empire, and so were well received as pilgrims. They made use of their opportunities through their music. Much of the Central European classic music of Liszt, Bartok, Dvorak, Verdi, and Brahms incorporated the Romani musical influence.

In Andalusia, Spain, the Romani and the Moors developed the flamenco guitar playing and dance as a disguised way of expressing their anger. This music is still popular in Spain and South America. In Hungary, Russia, and Slovakia, Gypsy folk songs are still sung. Charlie Chaplin, the entertainer, claimed Romani ancestry. Mother Teresa, Picasso, and Ava Gardner were also part Gypsy.

The U.S. Romani date back to precolonial times, but the largest numbers arrived in the late nineteenth and early twentieth centuries, when the United States opened its door to skilled people. "This was the opening for my great-grandfather, because he was a musician and my family members could make string instruments," remembers Bill. "In this country our musicians played European music and also developed their own style."

But the persecutions in Europe did not end. By 1895, Germans were using Gypsies for medical testing. The doctors would cut off a hand to see how long it would take the person to bleed to death. They had developed various dyes, and they injected these into the eyes of children to see if the dyes would change their color. None of these people survived. The Germans continued similar experimentations in the concentration camps that they set up primarily for Gypsies as early as 1927, years before World War II. Some of the doctors doing these experimentations were Jews.

Bill can't understand why Gypsies are not mentioned when the Holocaust story is told. They were dispossessed of property, jewelry, and all personal belongings. They were interned, tortured, and murdered in camps at Dachau, Ravensbruk, and Buchenwald. Romania had its own camps, and eventually expelled thousands of Gypsies to western Ukraine, where most of them died of disease, starvation, and brutal treatment.

In Serbia in the fall of 1941, German firing squads killed almost the entire male Gypsy population. In Hungary both Germans and Hungarians killed or deported Gypsies in 1944. "What is difficult," says Bill, "is the lack of research on their fate. Scholarly estimates of their genocide range up to one and a half million."

The Nazi regime viewed Gypsies both as asocials (outside "normal" society) and as racial inferiors, and believed they threatened the biological purity and strength of the "superior Aryan" race. This put them in the same category as Jews.

What gives Bill hope is that twentieth-century Romani have organized into political, social, and cultural groups to become self-determined. The International Romani Union has been a member of the United Nation's Economic and Social Council since 1979. In the late 1980s, it joined the United Nations Children's Fund (UNICEF) and belongs to the U.N.'s Educational, Scientific, and Cultural Organization (UNESCO).

In 1990 the European Romani Parliament was formed of professionals, educators, politicians, journalists, and political activists. The Romani have forged links with India, from where they originally migrated, and since the 1970s, the Indian Institute of Romani Studies has been researching the history, migration, and survival of the Romani.

"I join with all these organizations to combat racism and stereotyping in the media," says Bill. "In particular I will do everything I can to obtain war crimes' reparations for the Romanis who were in the Holocaust. This dedication is giving great meaning to my life."

Where is justice
when people are aggrieved
century after century,
dignity violated,
life destroyed?
Where is the balm of justice
to heal the wounds?

TIME FOR IDENTITY

If we do not know who we are or where we come from, we float in an ocean of space. Flouncing through life we seek this and that, rarely settling on what seems to fit our personality and needs. Connecting with the generations that have gone before us gives us stability and direction: we have a compass to guide us to our destination.

Our identity forms from our parents, our culture, and our education, and becomes clarified as we make our own decisions concerning the values in our lives. We are foolish when we reject past generations, who have garnered wisdom from their experiences that they pass on to their offspring.

Yet we cannot be trapped within our limited horizons, for we too need to pass on new vistas to the next generations. Even though tradition invites us to follow certain paths, we still need to explore for and by ourselves. Then our identity is distinguishable from that of others, even though we are inextricably a part of the whole. Then we have owned our true self.

His father was a Mayan, a healer of bones and muscles. His mother, of Spanish descent, was also a healer who used herbs. They married in Mexico and eventually migrated to New Mexico, where José was born.

The father believed that all life was religion and that those who came into one's life were part of that religion. He inculcated in José that attitude, as well as the importance of the culture that was their heritage. José learned early that this culture was rooted in two words: love and pain. "Everyone within this culture has to learn how to love who they are, where they came from, and how they speak. The culture teaches us to love our religion, our land, our neighbors, our adobe churches and homes, and most of all, our families."

The experience of his culture forged José's character because his ancestors had survived the pain of being not only the conquerors but also the conquered, of being the inquisitors as well as the prisoners, of being the landowners and then the dispossessed. His people had been overseers as well as workers, saints as well as sinners. They were born and buried with hymns, chants, and prayers. Violent deaths had been marked by wayside crosses.

"Our culture requires an understanding and acceptance of the sacrifice of the cross, of making sense of Abraham's willingness to sacrifice his son," he says. "It also remembers the roots of Aztec civilization that worshiped the sun and offered human sacrifice. How different is it from the American culture, which requires sacrificing of its young on foreign killing fields to preserve its freedom? That freedom also needs to allow the freedom for Hispanics to speak both English and Spanish in the United States.

"I am very secure about who I am because I know my race and culture. So long as one of our hijitos (children) understands our history, language, and faith, there is hope for families to be healthy, to maintain self-respect, and through their work, to contribute to the community and society.

"Love and pain. I love my family and my people. For them and because of them, I am able to sustain the pain of living life in the present while enjoying the sweet fruits from trees long ago planted by our forefathers and foremothers, who toiled and tilled the soil that yields our culture."

Finding a disparity among Hispanics in the States in recognizing and honoring their culture, José is devoting his life to reaching both youths and families, hoping to bring back the pride that is their inheritance. He has taught in schools, lectured to organizations and teachers, served on boards, challenged governments, and encouraged parents to preserve the culture belonging to them because they are Hispanic.

"I believe this is the time to keep that which has been passed down through generations, even though we are immersed in another culture. I consecrate my life to this vision, for the future exacts it."

Life is a journey giving us opportunities
to explore the boundaries of our identities,
examining, investigating, discovering
that which is of parent and that which is of self.
The search is both frightening and buoyant.
Shaping us are failures and successes,
desperation and sanguine expectations.
We are rooted in one certainty—
the palm of God's hand caresses us
as it guides us to fulfillment,
sustaining our efforts to become true children of the Creator.

I am a Muslim, but for many years that did not mean much to me," says Atis. Born in Palestine, in one of the first cities to be occupied by the Israelis in 1948, within a year he and his family had moved to the refugee camps in Jordan. The conditions were harsh, and after seven years they moved again, this time to Saudi Arabia, where they lived for twelve years. Atis completed high school there. Recognizing that he had only a slender chance of a college education, because Saudi students had priority, he returned to Jordan.

"I had a Jordanian birth certificate because no certificate had been issued at my birth during the crisis in Palestine. My chances for the education I wanted in Jordan were as slim as those in Saudi Arabia. In 1986 I decided to go to the United States. I received my degree in electronic engineering from the University of Wisconsin at Stevens Point.

"At first I was caught up in the looseness I found on the college campus, drinking and partying like everyone else. Then Alice, my girlfriend, became pregnant, and I heard the wake-up call. I was trying to fit into a culture that wasn't mine. I could see the right path for me was to return to my religion, which guides every segment of my life."

Alice and Atis were raising the child as Alice was completing her studies to become a Muslim. Muslims believe everyone is born a Muslim, but that some abandon Islam to become Jewish or Christian. When a person recognizes this abandonment and decides to return to Islam, this is called "reversion," reverting to the original state.

Alice reverted to Islam during Ramadan. She follows Islamic practice: she wears Muslim clothes and submits to the rules of the Quoran. Being in touch with other American women who have become Muslims gives her some idea of what reversion entails. Atis and Alice were married in a mosque before the end of that Ramadan.

Being a Muslim for Atis means accepting the Quoran and the Sunnah (teaching) of the prophet Muhammad as the ultimate authority on matters of faith and practice. To Atis the Quoran is the word of Allah (God), as important as the Torah of Moses for Jews and the Gospel of Jesus for Christians. However, because the Jewish and Christian followers were corrupted by their societies, Allah gave the Quoran to Muhammad, the last prophet, to restore the purity of divine guidance.

Says Atis: "It is important to note that the Quoran is written in Arabic and needs to be studied and read in that language. Translations into other languages corrupt the message, and Muslims will not accept translations." The book is revered so much that it is never laid on the ground or permitted to touch filthy substances. Before entering a mosque, Muslims remove their shoes and kneel on small carpets so they will not dirty the floor.

"From their early years, children are taught to memorize and recite the Quoran word for word. To have memorized it perfectly is a sign of spiritual excellence. The verses are printed in elegant calligraphy, and frequently these verses adorn the walls and facades of mosques. Our book, the size of the Christian New Testament, is divided into one hundred fourteen *suras* (chapters), which are arranged according to their length, with the longest first. It is these chapters we memorize."

Muhammad, the prophet, received the Quoran from Allah. "We are not worshipers of Muhammad, and object to that implication. We worship and pray to Allah. *Islam* is an Arabic word meaning submission, surrender, or commitment. It is this submission that governs our lives.

"There are over one billion people throughout the world who follow this faith, even though many are not Arab. The largest Muslim populations are in Indonesia, but there are also large numbers in Pakistan, India, Bangladesh, Malaysia, China, the Philippines, Taiwan, Egypt, and Jordan. We have no specific recruitment policy to gain members, but we do not hide our faith. We utilize the media through newsletters, magazines, and television to let the world know about it. The costs are funded by the Gulf States."

Accepting Islam's responsibilities gives a Muslim identity, a sense of belonging to God. The Quoran regulates every aspect of political, social, and private life as to dress, manners, food, marriage, and duties owed to God and society. Islam classifies the actions outlined in the Quoran as obligatory, meritorious or recommended, indifferent (not meriting reward or punishment), reprehensible and disapproved, and forbidden (meriting punishment).

The five pillars of Islam are the external signs of adherence to the community and the will of God. Practicing the five pillars identifies Muslims with the community of Islam. The first pillar is the repetition of the belief, "There is no God but one God and Muhammad is his prophet." The second pillar requires praying five times daily. The third pillar is almsgiving, whereby the believer is required to give a fixed percentage of his property for the poor and the wayfarer. The fourth pillar is the observance of Ramadan when all, except those who are ill, pregnant, or aged, fast for an entire month, refraining from food and drink from dawn to sunset. The fifth pillar is the Hajj, a journey to Mecca, where Muhammad received the Quoran.

Atis rejects one stereotype about Muslim identity. "We are sometimes called terrorists. The Quoran does not teach us to hurt others, but it does teach us to fight for our freedom and our faith. We do this through protests, throwing stones, and even suicide and guns when necessary. However, it does not allow us to kill civilians and foreigners as the radical Egyptians are doing. When Hamas attacks the Israelis, it is fighting for the freedom of the Palestinians, for no one else fights for them.

"I recognize I have been indifferent to the instructions of the Quoran, but want to surrender myself to them once more. This will give me peace and the certainty I am accepting my responsibilities before Allah." For Atis, a return to Islam is a return to his true identity.

Born to homogeneity
gives meaning to a person's identity.
Twists and turns of the wider world
challenge, maybe subvert, but
can lead to a glad return
to that which was and is to be.

What does it mean to be Jewish? If you would have asked me a decade ago, I don't know what I would have said. It was not something I thought about, or felt strongly about, until the beginning of the nineties."

Richard was born to Jewish parents in the mid-forties in New Jersey. The family moved often. Before he was out of high school, he had lived in Denver, Colorado; Park Forest, Illinois; Wilkes-Barre, Pennsylvania; Baltimore, Maryland; Syracuse, New York; Pittsburgh, Pennsylvania; and Columbus, Ohio. "Only once did we live in a neighborhood where there were very many Jewish families, and that was in a suburb of Baltimore. Looking back, I can see that even with my limited 'Jewishness,' I felt a part of that group."

The Jewish faith meant little to Richard before he was nine years old. "We actually had a Christmas tree until I was about six. After that it was a Christmas tree and a Hanukkah menorah. By the time I was eight years old, we celebrated only Hanukkah. At that time my parents told me a little about being Jewish and why we didn't celebrate Christmas."

In Wilkes-Barre Richard attended Hebrew school for one year. The family moved a few more times before he was thirteen, but he never had a bar mitzvah. While in Baltimore he attended a Reform Temple with his family. There was no celebration of the Sabbath at home.

"When I was in the seventh grade, a student who was fascinated by World War II gave a report that glorified Germany, Hitler, and his war effort. This was the first time I had heard about the Holocaust or seen any pictures about it. I couldn't believe people treated other people that way, just because of their religion.

"When I came home and told my parents about the report, they told me not to let anyone know I was Jewish. They made it clear the Holocaust wouldn't happen in this country as it did in Germany, but that there were people here who didn't like Jews, so it was safer to keep quiet about it."

In college Richard rarely dated Jewish women, and for a while he was married to a Catholic. They moved to Minnesota. While neither practiced their faith, they did celebrate Hanukkah and Christmas.

After his divorce in his middle thirties, Richard made a conscious decision to return to his Jewish roots. Eventually he married Marian, a Jewish woman, and they have been slowly building a Jewish life and home for themselves.

The three branches of Judaism faced Richard with a choice. Reform is the more liberal branch; Conservative, a traditional form; and Orthodox, the most unchanging. "I understand the Orthodox Jews are attuned to a strict adherence to the six hundred thirteen laws, or commandments, God gave his children more than fifty-seven hundred years ago in the desert.

"When I was examining my roots, I realized I wasn't interested in Orthodox or Conservative Judaism. Marian and I joined a Reform Temple, for we enjoyed their liberal views toward the equality of men and women, their alternate lifestyles, and their social-action involvement. But the internal politics became too messy for us, so we left.

"After wandering around in the Minneapolis–Saint Paul 'desert' for somewhat less than forty years, we discovered a smaller branch of Jewish beliefs and traditions. We found Jewish Renewal. This offshoot was started by Rabbi Zalman Schachter-Shalomi, who is an ordained Hasidic rabbi and has studied with a number of Eastern and Western theologians.

"He has taken traditions from different branches of Judaism and developed a way of celebrating Jewish life that treats women and men as equals, and combines music, dancing, singing, *davvening* (prayer), the study of the Torah, mysticism, and meditation into a type of spirituality that made us feel at home during the first service we attended. This is a joyous branch, and often we meet in people's homes to celebrate the Sabbath together, to read and discuss the Torah, and to celebrate our numerous holidays."

Since Richard has returned to his Jewish heritage, he has been at peace with himself. While driving through the Jewish cemetery at his mother-in-law's funeral, he was looking out the car window at the gravestones. "As I read the Jewish names and recognized the symbols, I felt a comfort, a connectedness I had rarely felt before. It was as if I was among family and friends. Although it was a very emotional and painful time, I felt at peace."

*As we struggle to find our own niche,
to leave our own imprint on the tablets of memory,
we mobilize our personal pasts
to accept and claim our uniqueness
in the hope of finding gladness and peace.*

TIME FOR ACCEPTANCE

Rejection's ache is insidious. It eats away our sense of self-worth, causing withdrawal and an abandonment of hope. Our rejection of others throws its weight around through our harsh judgments, sarcasm, disrespect, censure, and various humiliations.

The commandment of love requires acceptance of each person, regardless of how we feel about his or her actions. It exacts respect and understanding. The Gospels are full of examples in which Jesus accepted the "refuse" of society: the poor, the forlorn, sinners, tax collectors, as well as publicans and Pharisees. How can we refuse to do likewise, especially to those whom we have labeled unfit?

Time for acceptance also means admitting our prejudices and acknowledging our weaknesses, which in turn may be rejected by others. God is the only judge who can read the heart to determine who is guilty or innocent.

Michael had always felt different as he was growing up, but he could not explain why. While in high school, he read about homosexuals, and because they were defined primarily in terms of sexual practices, he was sure he was not one of them. In late adolescence he struggled with emotional attractions to other males. "These were so strong that I didn't know what to do with my heart."

The Christian beliefs that he had learned told him that homosexuality was wrong, so he repressed some of the physical attraction, but could not deal with the emotional component. By the end of his college years, he was able to acknowledge that he was gay, and told his parents. They were tremendously supportive.

Ever since he was a child, Michael had felt attracted to the church and had wanted to become a priest in the Episcopalian tradition. Even though he was gay, he decided to enter the seminary. This yearning for ordained ministry was the risk he took, because he believed it was acceptable to be gay and celibate.

While in seminary he dated six or seven other gay men. Then he began a serious relationship with a seminarian. They have been partners ever since. Michael says, "Though we knew our church was not accepting of gay seminarians or pastors in relationship, still we both felt that through our love, we experienced profoundly the love of God." They knew that they would face future struggles, but were willing to take the risk. "In fact, we believed our call to love each other was primary and our call to serve the church secondary."

Two years later they had a service of holy union, and among the thirty people attending were two ordained faculty members and Michael's internship supervisor. In a year both partners were ordained and received calls to the same diocese.

Michael's first church in Chicago was known for its ministry to gay people. He was at peace because he could be open with this congregation. Michael had no intention of making an issue of it, and even though his congregation intuitively knew he was gay, he never publicly announced it. He also knew his bishop was quietly supportive.

When Michael's partner got an important call to Detroit, Michael chose to leave his beloved church. "It was the hardest thing I have ever done." Because he could not announce to the congregation why he was leaving, he let them know he was continuing his studies in Detroit. He did not have a position when he arrived, so he did a combination of part-time jobs.

His pastoral colleagues in Detroit know that he is gay, and Michael has told a handful of persons, all of whom are supportive. But he feels it is inappropriate to come out publicly because official Episcopalian policy forbids relationships for gay pastors. "At times I wonder why I choose to live this way. Wouldn't it be better to 'come out' and not live a double life? That is tempting, but the church has been the center of my life and I cannot imagine walking away from it." So he struggles.

Michael is certain that in time the policies of the church will change. "I guess I'm ahead of my time. I'm hoping for the day when I can come out to my past and present congregations. I feel that in the future my story may serve an important purpose for the church as it acknowledges gay pastors as well as their gifts and lifelong relationships."

While in Chicago, Michael's congregation had quietly provided blessings for gay relationships, and he had presided at eight of these. The Episcopalian congregation Michael serves in Detroit is exploring this same possibility. He believes that there cannot be a double standard, one for straight couples and another for gay ones. "Sometimes I am impatient, and I weep as I yearn for justice and understanding. On the other hand, I am grateful to have been ordained to use my gifts in ministry while I am in a committed relationship, even if it is lived quietly and out of the public eye."

Acceptance brings security,
guaranteeing honor and equity.
It is a warranty
endorsing the worth of another.
Yet life situations can disqualify
a portion of humanity
by excluding, ostracizing, prohibiting
total membership in the human race.

Bob doesn't remember ever being interested in girls. In high school he began wondering if he was different from other boys. In college he made friends with three gay men and was finally able to admit that he, too, was gay. "I was born that way." He never told his parents. His father died of a heart attack without knowing of his son's lifestyle. "Mother has Alzheimer's disease. If I told her, would she understand?"

Today Bob is struggling with HIV. He is not able to identify who infected him. "I lived with a partner for five-and-a-half years. It was a love relationship that focused on more than just sex. After my partner left, the one-night stands that followed were nothing but giving in to my sex drive."

The diagnosis came around Christmas when Bob was fifty-six years old. He was told that he had an outside chance of living five years. He contemplated suicide because he was so depressed, but didn't have the courage to do it. "I was lonely and fearful of letting anyone know my condition. The public is so ignorant of HIV, I was certain I would be rejected if I 'came out.' Grappling with these fears, I went to a psychiatrist for help."

Bob lost forty pounds, became ashen gray with sunken cheeks, and his T-cell count dropped to 150, way below the 1,000 count that was normal. He developed an abnormality of the nervous system in his extremities. His toes and soles tingle constantly; the pain keeps moving up his legs. He also has borderline diabetes and respiratory problems. Fatigue is constant, requiring periods of extra rest daily.

As treatments improved, Bob started a special diet and was taking a cocktail of six pills daily: a Pro-tease inhibitor and Invirase, plus two Zerit and two Epivir. He was getting massages, reflexology, and acupuncture treatments weekly, and was visiting a subspecialty center bimonthly. His blood count became normal, and his previous outward physical symptoms disappeared. A nasalscopy revealed no lung cancer, and an endoscopy confirmed that he did not have throat, stomach, or intestinal cancer. He has also had heart stress tests that indicate no abnormality.

Because of the disease, Bob has researched the subject of homosexuality thoroughly. "I am comforted in knowing there is a genetic tendency toward homosexuality and that there was no choice on my part for that lifestyle. There is also a positive side to it, for homosexuals tend toward gentleness and nonviolence."

Bob is aware that his immune deficiency will betray him, but he has outlived the five years given him. "I should have been a vegetable by now, but my health seems to be improving. My T-cells have risen from 150 to 700, and I expect to reach the normal, healthy 1,000." However, that has brought its own problems. Bob's finances are dwindling. He no longer has the strength to manage a home, so he has to reprogram his body and mind.

Nevertheless, as he recalls his past, Bob says, "I have led a full life." He was drafted to fight in the Korean War. After leadership training, he was sent to Alaska for additional training, where he was involved in mock battles in 25- to 30-degrees-below-zero weather, hauling heavy weapons "just like huskies." Eight men lived in a tent set up in snow two to three feet deep. Because of the damage the constant gun barrage inflicted, to this day Bob has a ringing in his ears. At first he was disappointed because he had not been sent to the front. In hindsight he sees his assignment to Alaska as a gift of providence, for he is doubtful that his nonviolent nature would have allowed him to kill anyone.

Upon his return to civilian life, Bob earned a master's degree in speech and theater on the G.I. Bill. He utilized these skills in several high school, college, and university programs, directing plays and forming drama groups. "I had a good relationship with the students." Indeed, Bob's greatest satisfaction in life was the time he spent in education. He remembers with amusement what his twelfth-grade English teacher told him: "You've no business going to college; your English grades are disgraceful. You'll never be accepted." That putdown became a challenge.

Bob still lives in his own home, certain he will get help from social agencies when it is needed. He has not joined any support groups because he is shy and reserved. Instead he copes with his problems on a one-to-one basis with those who are compassionate and understanding. "I look forward to my weekly reflexology sessions with Bette, my reflexologist. She knows how to listen, and she comforts me, helping me set goals for the rest of my life." Bette, too, looks forward to these sessions and enjoys Bob's sense of humor.

His house looks like a small museum, for during the past twenty years, Bob has collected treasures from England, Italy, Germany, and China. Because he also helps with estate sales, he has acquired some antiques. Time is running out for him, so he struggles with their relinquishment. "Bette has convinced me I can't take any of these treasures with me. Should I donate them? will them to somebody? Should I have an estate sale and, with the proceeds, travel while I am still strong enough?" These serious decisions concern him.

"I still have time to fulfill some of my dreams. I need to leave a legacy, and want to do that with a written and pictorial account of our family tree. Some years ago, when we were on a family tour in Germany, I began my search of German family records. Now I feel an urgency to finish it."

Bob likes traveling to Germany, especially during Advent. "Life is filled with animation and magic. In the *Weihnachtsmarkt* (Christmas markets) the stalls are trimmed in pine boughs; the children walk in lantern processions. There is plenty of *Gluhwein* and bratwurst. What a simple, touching life it is! That's the star I need to follow.

"My days are pretty lonely at times, and I wonder what it would have been like to have a family. If I had one, would any member be willing to care for me? I know that speculation does me no good, but I still wonder. Yet I feel life would have been satisfying if I would have had a lifelong partner instead of the short-term one I had.

"I think of death and know none of us can escape it, but it will come soon for me. I used to fear it, but that fear has diminished. Bette has helped me see it is but a doorway to another level of life. She has also pointed out that my intense desire to celebrate Christmas in simple towns in Germany is a symbol not only of Christ's birth but also of the birth I am awaiting. I don't know what to expect, but I am sure it will be the ultimate evolvement."

Coming out claims one's difference,
but leaves an opening
to be declared unclean, tarnished.
But liberation comes in claiming authenticity,
by banishing, repudiating condemnation.

After raising a family of five children, Lee and Ron decided they would spend their retirement years as volunteers, in order to give back to others some of the blessings they had received themselves. They set about locating a place they could serve, and after exploring possible opportunities, they decided to visit five locations before making a decision.

Their first trip took them to Tampa, Florida. Here were three homes for mentally challenged women. A guardian invited Lee and Ron to attend a New Year's Eve party that these women had prepared. Even though they were not too interested, they decided to go. The warmth with which they were greeted impressed them. Everything at the party had been prepared by the women, and their joy was evident.

"Our decision to remain in Florida," says Lee, "happened during the party. The residents spontaneously started singing carols without concern for key or sound. In spite of the dissonance, it seemed to me they were praising God with their cacophony and sending us a message that this was where we belonged."

This party resolved their search. Lee and Ron became house managers for eight women who had lived together for ten years. For fifteen months they were "Mom" and "Dad" for women ranging from thirty to sixty years of age. They transported, shopped with, and entertained their "family" six days a week, twenty-four hours a day. They only left when a permanent couple took over.

"We were touched daily by the unconditional love these women gave us," notes Lee. "There were occasional confrontations, but love always saw us through. The simplicity of their prayers before meals helped us realize God is just as satisfied with faltering petitions as with liturgical praise."

After living with this "family," Lee and Ron recognize that God does not love these challenged children any less than "normal" children. Ron adds: "God has blessed them in many ways, for they can love just for the day and can forgive easily. They enjoy the simplest daily occurrences. We were able to interact with the residents as friends and accept them at face value. We enjoyed life with them as it happened daily."

In hindsight Lee is convinced God led them to this location, even though they were eager to visit other places. "We were directed to Florida first," she says. "It was only later we found out that one of the resident's mothers had been praying for two years for someone to come. She told us that as soon as she saw us, she knew we were the answer to her prayers."

God challenges us to accept others
as we have been accepted by the Creator.
This request, coming from the Godhead,
merits endorsement to ally ourselves with love.
To receive the disadvantaged, lonely, alienated, and poor
as cordially as the affluent and the successful
verifies the value of all humanity
as members of the family of God.

TIME FOR LOVE

In the life of any faith-filled person, there is always time for love. Love wells up when we perceive needs others might have. Love pours out mercy, tolerance, and good. Love opens its heart and offers its hands in service wherever it is needed. When one loves, generosity and unselfishness flow as graces to others.

God scattered messages throughout both the Hebrew Scriptures and the Christian Testament that identify the kind of love God offers us. God loves all humanity and each of us personally. God declares, "The mountains may depart and the hills be removed, / but my steadfast love shall not depart from you" (Isaiah 54:10). Yahweh tells Jeremiah, "I have loved you with an everlasting love; / therefore I have continued my faithfulness to you" (31:3). More powerfully still, Yahweh reaffirms to Hosea, "I desire steadfast love and not sacrifice" (6:6).

Jesus told his followers, "Love your enemies and pray for those who persecute you" (Matthew 5:44). He also spelled out what kind of behavior is expected of the one who loves. When the scribe asked him which commandment is the most important, Jesus replied, "You shall love the Lord your God with all your heart. . . . The second is this, 'You shall love your neighbor as yourself.' There is no other commandment greater than these" (Mark 12:30–31).

To emphasize the power of love, at the Last Supper, Jesus reiterated the two great commandments and then proved that love by dying for our redemption the next day: "I give you a new commandment, that you love one another. Just as I have loved you, you also should love one another" (John 13:34). Paul adds to this description of love in many places in his letters. One of the most eloquent exhortations is in 1 Corinthians 13:1, "If I speak in the tongues of mortals and of angels, but do not have love, I am a noisy gong or a clanging cymbal."

Day by day through each act, we determine the depth of our love for God, for others, and for ourselves.

On her seventieth birthday, Rita Steinhagen, a Sister of Saint Joseph of Carondelet, along with twenty-one others, was sentenced to six months in a federal prison and fined three thousand dollars by Judge Bob Elliott, the same judge who had sentenced Martin Luther King Jr. decades before and pardoned William Calley for his part in the My Lai massacre. Rita had crossed the white line leading to the School of the Americas (SOA) in Fort Benning, Georgia.

Before sentencing on 21 January 1998, each person to be sentenced had an opportunity to speak. Rita began her statement to the judge: "I am a Sister of Saint Joseph of Carondelet, and I am proud to say that ten members of my community are here today to support me.

"I'd like to begin with a quote from Archbishop Desmond Tutu. He states: 'If you are neutral in situations of injustice, you have chosen the side of the oppressor. If an elephant has his foot on the tail of a mouse and you say you are neutral, the mouse will not appreciate your neutrality.'

"I am here today because I don't want to be neutral. I am here because I know of the great injustices inflicted on the people of those small countries of Latin America. I have lived in Nicaragua and Guatemala, and I have seen firsthand the suffering of the people. I am also here for the four American churchwomen who were raped and murdered in El Salvador in 1980. Of the five officers cited for those crimes, three were graduates of the School of the Americas in Fort Benning, Georgia.

"For many years our government has sent money to those countries in Latin America so their soldiers could come to the United States for military training at the School of the Americas. Their training, which was described in manuals released by the Pentagon—after a bit of pressure—in 1996, recommended interrogation techniques like torture, execution, blackmail, and arrests of family members.

"The graduates of the school are notorious for their cruelty, often killing outright after first raping and torturing. One article stated, 'There has been a trail of blood and suffering in every Latin American country where School of the Americas' graduates have returned.' An editorial in the New York Times in September 1996, concluded, 'An institution so clearly out of tune with American values should be shut down without delay.'

"For over two years, I have worked with clients from the Center for Victims of Torture in Minneapolis. More than four hundred thousand victims of torture live in the United States; approximately twelve thousand live in Minnesota. These clients come from all over the world, and some of them come from countries whose military personnel have been trained at the School of the Americas. I have seen their marks of torture, and I have heard their stories.

"How can I remain neutral? How can anyone remain neutral when they know such a place as the School of the Americas is causing such pain and suffering to so many people in so many countries? It is beyond the time to shut the place down.

"And one more thing, Your Honor. Today I am celebrating my seventieth birthday. I have never been in prison, but I want to tell you that from what I have seen and heard in this courtroom the last couple of days, the fact that peaceful protesters can get six months in a federal penitentiary is more scary to me than going to prison."

This was not the first time that Rita had been at Fort Benning. A year earlier she had marched in the procession and had stepped across that white line. Because it had been her first "offense," she had received a ban-and-bar letter, forbidding her to cross that line for the next five years. "How could I obey it when I know the abominations committed by the graduates of the School of the Americas? About sixty thousand Latin American officers have been trained here."

There were two thousand people outside the entrance on 16 November 1997, the anniversary of the murder of the eight Jesuits, their housekeeper, and her daughter in El Salvador in 1989. Among the protesters were teachers, social workers, musicians, students, retired business executives, and carpenters. Six hundred and one people entered the base, each carrying a white plyboard cross, one-and-a-half-feet high. Each cross bore the name of someone who had been killed or had disappeared in a Latin American country. Eight coffins, commemorating the Jesuits, their housekeeper, and her daughter, preceded the procession. The coffins contained thousands of signatures requesting the closing of the School of the Americas. Rita was carrying Dorothy Kazil's cross. Dorothy was one of four churchwomen raped and murdered in El Salvador on 2 December 1980.

Months earlier Rita had been in Washington, D.C., with two hundred people sitting on the Capitol steps, protesting the training at the school. The following day they went to the Pentagon for a procession around that building. Rita was a bit late, and when she arrived, crosses had already been distributed. A woman who had two crosses gave her one. The name on it was that of Dorothy Kazil. The procession was led by a person dressed as Uncle Sam, who was followed by those dressed as peasants with the signs of their countries. Alongside them were men dressed as soldiers in fatigues, carrying cardboard guns. Everyone else carried a cross. All marched to the slow cadence of a drumbeat.

"We marched around the Pentagon and stopped at the lawn in front," remembers Rita. "The peasants knelt down, and the soldiers with their cardboard guns 'shot' them, while some of the marchers dug shallow graves in the lawn and buried the 'dead.' Those of us watching left our crosses planted on the front lawn. We resumed at the Capitol, where Roy Bourgeois, the Maryknoller who had organized the demonstration, asked those who wished to share their feelings about the event to do so.

"One person told of the Pentagon employee who had been watching the procession. As the marchers passed, he had said, 'I know; I understand; I'm with you, but I have a family to feed.' One of the marchers responded, 'So did the people who were murdered.'"

Rita then told the group: "I was very touched to receive the cross with Dorothy Kazil's name on it. Many of us had watched the television reports years ago when the bodies of the four murdered women had been uncovered from their shallow graves in El Salvador. When I saw re-enacted the digging of shallow graves at the Pentagon, it was very moving. I left Dorothy Kazil's cross planted at the Pentagon." Then someone in the crowd said, "Here, hand her this." The person who had picked up Kazil's cross from the Pentagon grass passed it down to Rita.

Rita kept it hung in her bedroom until she brought it with her to Fort Benning. She lost it there when the crosses were placed in the coffins and the SOA administration confiscated the coffins for evidence. "I have a picture of it though," says Rita. "That photo will have to take the place of the cross."

Rita is no stranger to life on the edge. When she was thirty-seven years old, she was diagnosed with multiple sclerosis, which affected two areas in her spinal cord and the base of her brain. She was troubled with it for eight years, but her MS has been in remission since then.

Before the diagnosis she had been a medical technologist working in hospital labs in Grand Forks and Jamestown, North Dakota. Expecting to be bound to a wheelchair for the rest of her life, she began scriptural studies, hoping she could teach. Having some trouble walking the campus, she left the college and moved to Minneapolis. Rita began exploring the streets of Minneapolis, getting acquainted with runaways, alcoholics, drug addicts, and homeless people. For five months she hung around street corners, getting to know the people.

Finally, the owners of an empty building on a corner nearby gave her the key to the building, because she had promised to keep it up. This became the Free Store. Here motorcyclists, people of color, cross-dressers, American Indians, and elderly people found clothing and household articles that they needed.

Soon another problem became evident to Rita. Runaways had no shelter. Eventually, after many negotiations, a boarded-up house was given to Rita rent free. With much help it was renovated and licensed. The University of Minnesota sent students for training and in-service. The Runaway House opened in 1972 and is still functioning.

Rita next went to Stillwater, Minnesota, and spent two years in a community of prayer. Returning to Minneapolis, she and two other Sisters of Saint Joseph started a Catholic Worker House for homeless women and children. They named it Saint Joseph's House. Today it is called Saint Joseph's Hope Community and encompasses a square block. It provides stable living conditions for families.

While studying Spanish in Texas, Rita met undocumented people coming in from El Salvador, Nicaragua, and Guatemala. "I joined Witness for Peace and went to Antigua, Guatemala, for four months, continuing my study of Spanish. Witness for Peace assigned me to northern Guatemala, and I lived with a widow for eight months as I worked in that area.

"I saw the devastation caused by the military both in Nicaragua and Guatemala. Later I learned these soldiers were trained by SOA. How can I stay away from joining the efforts to close the School of the Americas?"

Rita's experiences in Central America have led her to work with the Center for Victims of Torture based in Minneapolis. "I am the rounder-upper, finding clothing, furniture, bedding, and whatever material things the clients need. I help them get established in homes, find them places of safety. Occasionally I help them fill out the forms that will help them find the housing they need."

When the clients at the Center found out about her sentence, they were fearful. All they could remember were their experiences in their own prisons, and the tortures that had brought them to the Center. "I told them it is not like that in our prisons, but it is hard for them to believe that," says Rita.

Rita has paid her fine and served her sentence in the minimum-security women's Federal Prison Camp in Pekin, Illinois.

The Spirit of the Lord is upon me,
because he has anointed me
to bring good news to the poor.
He has sent me to proclaim release to the captives
and recovery of sight to the blind,
to let the oppressed go free,
to proclaim the year of the Lord's favor.
(Luke 4:18–19)

When Bette was working with AIDS patients and orphans in Haiti, with Mother Teresa's Missionaries of Charity, she learned what it means not to be judgmental. Walking down a rocky road one day, she fell and held out the palm of her hand to protect herself. Expecting a sharp stone to rip open her palm, she was surprised at the smooth, heart-shaped stone she picked up. As she clutched it, she distinctly heard the words, "I will take your heart of stone and turn it into a heart of flesh." She remembers this powerful promise whenever she is tempted to judge another person.

From early adulthood Bette had determined not to live a superficial or boring life. As a Christian she sought to base her work on the Scriptures, which sent her messages that her eyes could see and her ears could hear.

Bette began her career of mercy when her husband was stationed on Treasure Island, San Francisco, during World War II. The first hospices in the United States were being set up, and as an act of love, she volunteered to work with the dying.

At war's end she and her husband, a pharmacist, moved to Saint Paul, Minnesota, where Bette began volunteering at Gillette Children's Hospital as a physical therapist. At the same time, she was working with dying cancer patients who were cared for by the sisters in Our Lady of Good Counsel Cancer Center. When her husband died, she was offered a full-time position at Gillette.

At the cancer center, Bette had listened to tapes describing the work of Mother Teresa's community. She learned there were fifty-two thousand volunteers working throughout the world in orphanages and clinics. She was impressed, but she had plenty to do where she was living.

Then one of the sisters in the cancer home invited Bette to go to Haiti as a volunteer for the Missionaries of Charity to work with people with AIDS. By now she had remarried, and was doubtful her husband, Dan, would approve. However, she mentioned the invitation to him. He surprised her by declaring that he would join her. Beginning in 1983 the two of them worked from Thanksgiving to Christmas for four years, living in a remodeled motel. Their first Thanksgiving they feasted on dried wieners and chips.

Bette and Dan washed the dying, fed them, and put them to bed in clean cots. Dan, who was a plumbing and heating expert, installed needed equipment. Communication was not difficult, even though the patients spoke Creole. The sisters knew English.

During one of their years in Haiti, they worked in an orphanage. "I remember the distended stomachs, the ribbed chests, and the swollen heads, sometimes larger than their stomachs. All this time, in spite of poverty and suffering, we sensed God's presence, and I felt very connected with God. Stumbling on that rocky road to find the stone heart was a gift I will always treasure. I still hear the words I heard then." Bette keeps that stone heart in a place of honor in her home.

"I remember the parable of Jesus wherein the rich man is condemned because he refused to help the poor man Lazarus. My life is dedicated to loving those whom the world rejects. I believe that when

I love, the Lord loves through me. I am convinced that when I decrease, God's power increases and spiritual miracles take place."

Love is patient;
love is kind;
love is not envious or boastful
or arrogant or rude.
It does not insist on its own way;
it is not irritable or resentful;
it does not rejoice in wrongdoing,
but rejoices in the truth.
It bears all things, believes all things,
hopes all things, endures all things.
Love never ends.
(1 Corinthians 13:4—8)

Eleven children were enough to keep Dorothy Coughlan at home caring for them. The oldest was twenty-one when the youngest was born. "I have memories of unending laundry, simple meals of hot dishes, constant chauffeuring, and years of sleepless nights. Ours was also a foster home for ten years, when we welcomed over one hundred children."

Even so Dorothy found time for church committees, adult Bible study, and teaching children's religious-education classes. She was chairperson for her diocese's Respect Life Committee, worked eight years with the League of Women Voters and twelve years with the Minnesota Citizens Concerned for Life (MCCL).

Dorothy and her husband, Dan, also found time for travel. "We enjoy seeing the world, and have traveled throughout Europe, Morocco, Turkey, Palestine, Mexico, Central America, Hawaii, and the Philippines." They went to Nicaragua for six weeks to learn from and work with Christian base communities.

"We don't like Minnesota winters, and don't want to sit around for three or four months. Since we desire to serve the poor in some capacity, we have been working in Mazatlan with Ayuda por Una Familia (Help for the Families), a local charity. Our primary task is to raise funds for the Colonia Genaro Estrado, a poor barrio of mostly women and children."

Dan does not speak Spanish, so his task is to take tourists to the Colonia to see the needs of the people. Here a day-care and learning center is staffed by two couples who have been trained by the Salesian fathers to work with uneducated youth. Dorothy also works with the children, helping them create art to be used on calendars and Christmas cards.

Dan's family has been associated with the Mankato building-stone industry for three generations. This industry quarries large blocks of stone from a proven stone formation and cuts the stones to fit an architect's design and texture.

A Jesuit's talk at a Newman Center on parents' rights in education convinced Dan that he needed to be involved in politics. "I became part of an organized pressure group and went to the Minnesota State Capitol to influence our legislators. Our first agenda called for a fair bus bill, which was passed. In the early seventies, we passed a tax-credit bill to help private schools." Because Dan had a number of children to educate, he worked eagerly on any proposal that helped the cause.

Both Dan and Dorothy are grateful for the influences and events in their lives. "I have never had a born-again experience," says Dan, "but I had parents who were good models for me. I accepted their ethics, their prayer life, and their beliefs. Now I pass on to my children that which was given to me so generously."

Dorothy has learned much from her own children and her foster children, and shares this wisdom with those who are less fortunate. "Working with poor people leaves me uplifted, happy, close to God. It's an opportunity for me to show my love for God and others. I take these opportunities as an indication that this is what God wants me to do at this time in my life."

Bearing good will to others
is a condition of the heart.
Its cordiality gives comfort
both to friends and strangers.

Tenderness and consideration
eliminate enmity and harassment,
for the enthusiasm to love
becomes the grace of devotion.

TIME FOR MINISTRY

The call, or vocation, to ministry is ours simply because of our creation with gifts, talents, desires, aspirations, and yearnings that surface throughout our lifetime. God loves us without reservation. Our response to God's unconditional love expresses our gratitude to the Creator by becoming God's presence in the world.

Becoming aware of existing needs and acknowledging that we too have insufficiencies can motivate us to balance discipling by both giving and accepting. Our cup then remains full, for as we empty ourselves, others replenish us. Sharing and receiving supplies the energy of the God-power to continue our lives of loving discipleship, our time for ministry.

As I read Ecclesiastes, I feel the 'time to keep and [the] time to throw away' reflects my journey," says Marie Luz. "I always had preconceived notions about what I was going to do with my life. In retrospect I acknowledge that God has asked me to abandon many of them so I could choose the road I otherwise would not have taken. Ironically I was convinced I had to keep sight of the gifts God had given me and try to use all of them."

Marie Luz's grandmother had been a healer, and Marie Luz strongly felt the call to be a doctor. She went from an inner-city high school to undergraduate study at Stanford University. Observing the premed students who were concerned mainly with their future earnings led her away from med school. She began preparing for ministry in public health.

After graduation Marie Luz found a job at a community clinic. She disliked the meetings, filling out reports and billings, and doing her boss's work. But she loved working with patients and finding community resources for them. She saw this desire as another bend in the road. Marie Luz applied to four medical schools, all of which accepted her.

Marie Luz attended Stanford Medical School. In her third year, she married Tom. When financial needs drove her to look for a part-time job, she found a research assistantship in geriatrics. She also found a mentor who cared about her, believed in her capabilities, and convinced her to accept a geriatrics fellowship after her residency in internal medicine.

About her internship at the county hospital in San Jose, Marie Luz says: "I learned people come in all sorts of packages, some that I had previously disdained. I hadn't wanted anything to do with IV-drug abusers, alcoholics, and prisoners." Marie Luz learned to be compassionate and to set aside her prejudices, and she became aware that the current choices she had made allowed God to be present in her life.

Toward the end of her geriatrics fellowship, Marie Luz applied for and received a grant to study determinants of skeletal health in elder Mexican American women. At the same time, she received an appointment to the Medical School faculty at Stanford. She was on her way to a high-powered career.

Then, while Marie Luz and her two children were visiting her parents in New Mexico, Tom was offered an excellent job in Seattle. She recalls: "Something about being with my parents enabled me to recognize that in spite of my academic career progress at Stanford, we needed to take this next step. I felt it was an invitation sent by God to rescue our marriage and our children, who were spending fifty hours weekly in day care."

Marie Luz finished her commitment to the grant by commuting from Seattle to Stanford for three years, and then took a year off. She tried to find a job, but finally realized God would send her something when she and her family were ready and when God needed her in some special arena.

Nine months after "retiring" from Stanford, Marie Luz received an invitation from the University of Washington's geriatrics division to join their long-term care program. This meant working in a nursing home. "For every reason I gave the recruiter for not wanting the job, he had an answer that removed all obstacles," Marie Luz remembers. Once again she saw God beckoning her to follow a path into the unknown, and this ministry has given her the opportunity to focus completely on healing.

Some years later Marie Luz's journey turned in another direction. She developed optic neuritis and lost half the vision in her right eye. Since this can be a symptom of multiple sclerosis, she asked everyone she knew to pray for her. Instinctively she sensed that MS would develop, despite the optimistic diagnosis of her doctor who told her the optic neuritis would clear up and that she was at low risk for developing MS.

Marie Luz went through all the stages of grief. When she felt most dejected and hopeless, she felt the power of all the prayers that were being said for her. "I had the sensation of being buoyed up by prayer. I felt the healing going on in my body, and I never again experienced that desperate feeling."

A year after the appearance of optic neuritis, the family went to the east coast for a baptism. During the trip her shoulders and jaw bothered her. She had a nagging feeling that MS had come to claim her. "The baptism took place in a tiny New England Episcopal church. The ceremony was one of the most spiritually uplifting times of my life. I could feel the presence of the Holy Spirit in the congregation surrounding that little baby.

"At the end of the Mass, after the rector made his usual announcements, he started back up to the altar, then turned, came down the stairs, and while fingering the tassel on the end of his rope belt, said, 'While I was praying earlier, it came to me that there is someone here today whose life is becoming frayed in some way, just like the end of this rope. I don't know if it is physical or not, but whoever it is needs our prayers. If that person feels comfortable coming up after the service to pray with the prayer group, please join us. If you are uncomfortable, we will still pray for you.' He turned and went back to the altar. The ceremony was over. I was in a daze. It was as if he were talking directly to me and had felt all my inner turmoil."

Marie Luz did not go up to the altar to join the prayer group. "The reason the family was gathered together was to baptize the newest member of our family. I did not want to channel that gloriously positive energy away from her. I knew MS was something I was going to have for at least a little while, whereas her baptismal day was going to happen just this once. I needed some time to pray and to gather my own spiritual energy so I could tell the rest of the family about my illness in a positive way. That incident in the New England church infused me with the strength I desperately needed at that point. I was able to be at peace with myself."

Life began to change for Marie Luz. Always so self-sufficient, now she felt the Spirit enabling her to ask for prayers from everyone, to invite others into her vulnerability, to share in her spirit. And Marie Luz believes that other people praying for her needs opened up their hearts also. Her brother returned to practicing his faith, and a girlfriend discovered the healing power of prayer, which brought back her son from a destructive lifestyle. "Tom learned how to pray. Roxanne, my daughter, had an opportunity to care for me, which brought us closer together spiritually. I was able to give up my pride and strength and accept the love of my family and friends."

Now in remission, this final stage of her healing took place when Marie Luz spent a month in New Mexico with her parents. "I needed to be a little girl again, to let them lay their hands on me, and to be pampered by them. I had always prayed for patience, and in MS God answered my prayer."

As she reviews her life, Marie Luz acknowledges that the dreams she had lain out for herself did not always come true, but in their stead, new paths led her to undreamed-of horizons. "I was wise when I surrendered to God's providence, for then I knew when to keep my dreams and when to throw them away."

Creator God, you invite me to discipleship,
but am I worthy? capable?
To be a disciple means to learn from the Teacher
and has nothing to do with worth or capability.
Are you implying that your invitation requires only
a heart open and trusting, a mind seeking truth,
a spirit free from fetters?
If I learn from you, will that knowledge make me uncomfortable

with what is comfortable in my life?
If I accept your image as being within me,
what demands will this make of me?
If I trust, will doubt dissolve, resistance turn to certainty?
Will my brokenness be made whole?
Will peace calm me?
No one else can say that "Yes" for me.
Inspire me to be insightful enough
to recognize your purpose for me
as I set my own purposes aside.
Take me as you have created me.
I come to you as I am.
Accept me as your disciple.

Almost thirty-seven years after he had begun training as an infantry officer at Fort Benning, Georgia, Bill Falvey returned to protest the presence of the School of the Americas. This school, run by the U.S. Army, trains Latin American military officers in "low intensity warfare," which includes such things as torture and assassination. Obviously Bill had gone through an enormous change in the intervening years.

During adolescence Bill did poorly in school, interested only in cars and girls. These feelings were compounded by the death of his father when Bill had just turned sixteen. After his father's death, two conflicting forces emerged and dominated his life: ambition and fear.

During his last year in high school, Bill's grades improved, and to the surprise of almost everyone, he graduated. However, the improved grades were insufficient to get him into Saint John's University in Collegeville, Minnesota. He wanted to go to Saint John's so badly that he drove there and persuaded the registrar to admit him as a freshman. After two years he transferred to the University of Minnesota, where he majored in political science. He enrolled in the ROTC program, and upon his graduation was commissioned a second lieutenant. The Army trained Bill as a counterintelligence officer and sent him to a posting in West Germany.

After two years in the Army, Bill returned home to begin law school. After graduation he was appointed assistant U.S. attorney. Because this was during the Vietnam War, one of his tasks was to prosecute draft dodgers. "I did this with the zeal of Saint Paul and a strong belief that our country was fighting 'godless Communism.' I assumed all young men, except cowards, would want to fight for their country."

Then Bill became a part-time assistant Ramsey County public defender, representing indigent people charged with criminal offenses. Five years later he became the first full-time chief public defender in Ramsey County. In ensuing years he was adjunct professor at William Mitchell College of Law. By the time he was in his early forties, Bill had accomplished most of the goals he had set for himself. Even so, with each new success came a "tightening grip of fear. All of these accomplishments satisfied my ego, but they also fueled my fear and insecurity."

To handle the fear, insecurity, and low self-esteem, Bill turned to alcohol and tranquilizers. Fear claimed the upper hand over ambition. "I had reached a point in my life where I knew what I was because I had an office wall adorned with diplomas, awards, certificates, and appointments, as well as a scrapbook full of newspaper clippings, but I did not know who I was." Eventually, with the help of a counselor and the support of a loving wife and children, Bill acknowledged he was an alcoholic and became a member of Alcoholics Anonymous (AA).

Bill underwent a change in other ways too. He had begun to believe that the government had lied about the war in Vietnam and its prolongation. At the same time, he renewed his interest in the church's teaching on social justice. As public defender he had come face to face with issues of poverty, sexism, and racism. His firm belief in the use of force in Vietnam began to waver. The new theology of liberation of Third World countries captured his imagination, and he began attending lectures on peace.

Bill helped in the defense of the protesters from the Minnesota Women's Camp for Peace and Justice. While protesting Sperry Rand's part in the manufacture of cruise missiles, the women were arrested for trespass. Despite the law the jury refused to convict them. Jury members saw them as remarkable women of peace and great courage.

Bill's journey next took him into the formation program to become a permanent deacon. Upon ordination he was assigned to Saint

Adalbert's parish in Frogtown, in the inner city of Saint Paul. There he helped form a partnering between two parishes and a Christian base community in San Rafael, Nicaragua. He traveled to Nicaragua. "It has given me a new vision of the injustice of poverty and the futility of violence."

Now Bill has Parkinson's disease. While cross-country skiing with his daughter, Kathleen, she noticed he had been dragging his left ski pole. This coupled with a tremor in his left hand led to a diagnosis of the condition. At first this illness was a mere inconvenience, but gradually it substantially affected his mobility, forcing a medical retirement. "I see a positive side to this illness, for it is an opportunity for spiritual growth. I have learned to trust God. It has also allowed me to meet many new and interesting people."

Bill continues as deacon at Saint Adalbert's, but he has dropped his work in the courts. However, he spends three mornings weekly at the Listening House, a drop-in center for street people.

Bill's life experiences have caused him to adopt a simple theology: love God and love your neighbor. "The concept of neighbor is not only local but also global. I believe all people are created in the image and likeness of God and all are entitled to be treated with love and justice and to be liberated from injustice. The culmination of my journey from 'hawk' to 'dove' after thirty years was my return to Fort Benning, where I had begun my military service. I have finally come 180 degrees. For that I am grateful, because my life has turned to the God of love. It has truly shifted, for the paralysis of fear no longer claims me."

The journey of many bends
may lead to dead ends,
or it may unveil broad highways,
which can become arteries of promise.
The wandering at times seems useless,
but following the route persistently
will lead invariably to gateways
opening up exceptional vistas.

Pregnant seven times herself, Janet Krocheski is fully aware of the privilege and the trauma of pregnancy. Three of her children were miscarried, and her daughter Mary was killed by a drunken driver at age twenty-three. The court charged the killer with careless driving and put him on a work-release program for sixty days.

Janet's faith was challenged. Her will kept her from losing it. She joined Mothers Against Drunk Driving (MADD) and worked three years with them. She talked to parents and at-risk children, discussing the issue of drinking and driving. Her personal feelings about justice for the victims of violent crime absorbed her. She did not believe in the death penalty, but she did believe that violent perpetrators needed to be put where they could do no more damage.

"Violence is never okay, and no mental gymnastics can ever excuse it. A stranger enters someone's life, does the damage, and leaves. The victims are left alone to deal with their anger, frustration, feeling of injustice, and the desire for revenge."

Janet lobbied the state legislature to pass a law to drop the legal alcohol level for drivers, and lost by one vote. She wonders if that one vote came from a legislator who callously asked her if passing that law would bring back her daughter.

About capital punishment Janet wrote: "Violent crime has risen tremendously in the past years, and people are mad. We all hurt when our young people are senselessly killed or injured. We all suffer when we become aware of another rape, beating, drunken-driving death, abused child, or battered woman. Our outrage increases when we realize that many of the criminals in these cases are repeat offenders who often have served only a few years or months for the same crime committed in the past. It is so unjust!

"I understand that feeling, having shared and experienced it. Our whole being screams out for justice. But justice is so elusive. In these cases there can never really be justice. Nothing, not even the execution of the criminal, can replace the loss or heal the wounds of the victims or their loved ones." And so Janet opposes capital punishment. "With all the pain, sorrow, suffering, and injustice in this world, I still believe in life. I believe that our Creator intends life to be good and a gift to be enjoyed by all.

"I know it is not always this way, for evil exists in our world and tears our lives apart. But life is still good. I believe that people were created for love, to share in this experience of life in beautiful and powerful ways. When we allow the legal execution of criminals, we suffer too. Each time it occurs, we become a little less than God intends us to be. We may think that 'justice is done' and now the victim has been vindicated or can rest in peace. But neither of these is true. Our loved ones do not rest more peacefully because their aggressors are dead. They will rest peacefully because they have returned to God who will heal them and make them understand."

Being pro-life led Janet to oppose the death penalty, but also to work for life. After the Supreme Court passed the Roe v. Wade law, Janet became actively involved in the pro-life movement. She became director of the Respect Life office of the Archdiocese of Saint Paul and Minneapolis to provide help to pregnant women. At first the focus was on crisis pregnancies. She was instrumental in setting up financial outreach programs and postabortion counseling.

Many Catholic women in crisis pregnancies expected reproach and blame rather than compassion and understanding. They stayed away from the source that should have been available to see them through the crisis. If they had had an abortion, their principal problem seemed to focus on forgiveness. "How can God forgive me? How can I forgive myself when I have terminated a pregnancy?"

Janet recognized the situation and worked with both priests and laity to develop an environment that would be compassionate and helpful. The focus was shifted from just abortion to all life issues, to any area where human life is threatened because of values and attitudes.

To help in this, Janet initiated the Marian Project that provided free, nonjudgmental help for women and men coping with the aftermath of abortion. This project is a network of qualified, caring volunteers who extend arms of acceptance to all women, the unborn child's father, the women's parents, and all who have been involved. This service is anonymous and is open to anyone, Catholic or not, for it is concerned with healing the pain and not with judging religious beliefs. Those who need professional assistance are referred to health-care professionals. All who feel guilt or shame, a sense of loss or grief, anxiety, anger, alienation, or depression are welcomed.

Janet has directed implementation of the pastoral letter "Abortion and a Failure of Community," calling all Catholics to respond as people of Jesus Christ to women and men who need support and the assistance of friendship during pregnancy or after children are born. The pastoral letter invited parishes to listen to women describe their experiences and needs during pregnancy and the raising of their children, and to reach out and respond to those needs with tenderness. Since its publication the vast majority of parishes in the archdiocese have responded. Volunteers have pledged to share community responsibility for changing a crisis pregnancy into a joyful occasion.

Four hundred coordinators in parishes have been trained to be responsible for their parish focus in this movement for A Community Caring for Life (ACCL). More than twenty thousand volunteers have committed themselves to help with day care, transportation to and from doctor appointments, housecleaning, providing a sympathetic ear, and financial help.

Janet feels like Moses looking upon a promised land. "Yes, I firmly believe in life, and so I'm deeply involved in this movement. I have heard the cry of the people, and believe God is calling me to this endeavor. If the future brings hope to the people in need, that will be enough."

At times it takes tragedy to shatter our dreams,
as with broken hearts we wander and wonder
what path God invites us to follow.
After our hearts, scarred with sorrow, stop their trembling,
we may find new horizons emerging in the distance.
In following the narrow road
leading to an unknown destination,
we may enjoy unexpected opportunities, new challenges.

TIME FOR GRIEVING

A time for grieving always follows the loss of that which we treasure: a loved one, a friendship, or a prized possession. Denying our grief only delays healing. Such denial leads to an infection of the mind, heart, and spirit, paralyzing activity. Healing of a broken bone takes time; so does healing a fractured heart.

Research has demonstrated the importance of tears in the process of healing. When we cry we drain the dross that is a barrier between suffering and healing. In addition tears cleanse, and in the cleansing, the relationship between Creator and creature can be made manifest. We realize who God is and who we are not. We lose our rigidity and sophistication. Instead we become more fully human, more in touch with the Divine. When we forget theology and analyses and let our heart draw close to God, the magnetizing power of God's love releases tears of sorrow, hope, joy, awe, healing, and gratitude.

In a little over six hours, life changed so drastically, I could not comprehend it. My son, Kevin, and I had dinner together at 5:00 p.m. that last day of the year, reminiscing about the past and planning for the future. He left to pick up Susie, his girlfriend, brought her back to her home around 8:30 p.m., and headed for a friend's house to bring in the New Year. By 10:30 Kevin was dead."

At a New Year's Eve party hosted by an adolescent boy, liquor was plentiful. The boy's father was a recovering alcoholic. Hanging on the wall was a framed copy of the Serenity prayer. Yet he provided the rum, the schnapps, and a keg of beer, charging five dollars per cup for those who wished to drink.

Kevin sampled it all in six-ounce shot glasses in the ninety minutes that he was there. He had more than twice the allowable limit.

113

Then he and his friend Roy took off. Kevin was speeding at fifty miles an hour on a roller-coaster road when he wrapped the car around a tree. He was killed instantly. Roy was critically injured and in a coma for a month, and underwent another month of therapy before being released.

Looking back Tom finds a bit of comfort in knowing Kevin had dropped Susie off at her home before going to the party. "I've reviewed everything that has happened over and over again. Kevin had gotten his driver's license just five days earlier. If I had not given him permission to take my car, would he be alive today? What value does his senseless death have? His friends have made a shrine of that tree, but I don't want it to remain so. Why glorify a death that didn't need to happen?"

The family hosting the party and supplying the liquor faced charges. The father served time in jail, and his son had to spend hours in community service so that he would not forget what he had done. Even so, one of the teens expressed what others felt: "What's the big deal? A lot of our parents do this. They would rather see us drinking in our own homes than in the homes of strangers."

Realizing this kind of reaction, and after discussion with his wife, Linda, and daughter, Kristin, the family decided to produce key rings that could be distributed to young people. The key ring carries the dates of Kevin's birth and death, and stamped in huge letters is the request, "Please DON'T drink and drive. Your friend, Kevin."

With the key ring comes a short description about Kevin and the reminder: "Kevin had heard all the warnings that you have heard. When alcohol is used, good judgment is not possible. The pain that is caused to friends and family when someone is killed is unbearable. It is a crime, and totally unacceptable to drink and drive. Don't do it!"

The reminder also encourages drivers to remember the pain they bring on those left behind. "Kevin was a wonderful son and brother. The pain and sadness that we now live with every day is unbearable. He had a future ahead of him, just as you do. Do not think you are indestructible. You are not. On behalf of parents everywhere, I beg you to think of others. Do not ever consider drinking and driving."

Tom wishes to make sense of Kevin's death. He has donated the wrecked car to Mothers Against Drunk Driving (MADD), who take it around to schools to show teenagers what can happen when they drink and drive. In addition Tom visits high schools and small groups to tell the story of Kevin's death. He passes a framed picture of Kevin around to the students, and after it returns to him, he passes around the death certificate and asks the teens to see their name there instead of Kevin's. He draws attention to the embossed seal that makes it official and final.

"I will never see my son again. His death was not necessary. I had always hoped Kevin would leave an impact on the world. I feel that it can still happen in ways that would not have been my choice. Even if only one of you doesn't drive when you have been drinking, his death will not have been in vain."

The heart is broken, ambushed by pain,
the ache a kind of martyrdom
as sorrow and distress lay claim.
Once the affliction is permitted an escape,
life gradually returns.
The future sends out its invitation
to complete the personal tasks still awaiting.

Tom's life seemed to be routine. Each morning as he got up, he said his favorite prayer: "Dear God, so far in life, I've done all right. I haven't gossiped or lost my temper. I haven't been greedy, grumpy, nasty, selfish, or over-indulgent. I'm really glad about that. But in a few minutes, God, I'm going to get out of bed, and from then on I'm probably going to need a lot of help. Thank you in Jesus' name. Amen."

Tom's father had been a model for him, even though there had not been any emotional closeness between them. Tom hugged his dad for the first time when his father was fifty. The shock of this touch broke something open, and before long the dad was hugging family members. Now Tom had become a model for his dad.

Tom worked on the railroad for five years, traveling between Needles, Albuquerque, Phoenix, and the Grand Canyon. Since his absence left a void in the family, he settled down as a mail carrier for the next thirty years. This also allowed him to serve his community as a volunteer fireman.

"One day my life collapsed," Tom says. "My son Mike was diagnosed with bone cancer after a routine examination for a tender shoulder. Additional tests revealed he had lung cancer also, already in the fourth stage of progression. Mike knew he wasn't going to make it, even with chemotherapy, because the cancer had already spread not only to his hips but also to his brain. He told his wife he did not want machines to keep him alive." Within a few months, he was quietly welcomed home by God.

For Tom and Darline, his wife, the loss of their son was devastating. They were grateful that he had not suffered too long, but the pain of loss hit them hard. In his grieving Tom remembered this fable he had heard about twins:

> The twins had to leave the womb of their mother when it was time for birth, but were afraid to abandon their environment because it was the only one they knew. They were also unsure about the identity of the mother whom they had never seen. One of the twins did not want to leave the womb because he was sure there could be no life outside it. The other wondered if there might not be another kind of life after the womb. As they waited out their time, they continued their speculations and arguments until it was time for birth.
>
> The twins cried when they were born into the light and coughed out fluid and gasped the dry air. They opened their eyes, and for the first time, saw the mother who cradled them in her arms. They were awestruck at the beauty that lay outside the womb. Where there had been darkness before, now there was light. The mother whose existence they had doubted touched them in a way they had not experienced before. And that touch was good. They were glad to have left the womb, for something new awaited them.

"When I heard this story before," Tom says, "it didn't make any special impact. When I recall it now, I can visualize Mike leaving the womb of his earthly life to enter into a Light that is new and beautiful. Even though tears still come, Darline and I are comforted knowing Mike has entered into this glorious and unimaginable Light."

Grief, razor-edged, bleeds emotions,
callously ignoring the torment such anguish prolongs.
Unpredictable, life brings disappointment
when least expected.
As it crushes
it becomes a depository of pain,
astonishing even the strong-hearted,
whose dreams burst like bubbles in the wind.

She stood beside the weed-strewn grave. Madeline had found it only because the cemetery office had recorded the name and the location. It was her first visit, even though her baby had died thirty-seven years ago. Now the yearning to visit her daughter overwhelmed her. So did the memories.

Madeline was in the hospital giving birth, growing drowsy from the anesthesia, when the nurse whisked the child away. She knew it was a girl, but she never saw her baby or held her in her arms. Her husband, Len, had, and it was he who had made the funeral arrangements. She could not stop grieving. Neither could she forget, nor forgive Len or the nurse.

Soon after, an irreparable distance grew between Len and Madeline. Even so, six other children followed, children she loved and hugged and touched. But her heart ached desperately for the little one who was gone. She had named her Therese Marie.

Madeline came across an anonymous article that gave her the stamina to keep going. She put it on her refrigerator and read it daily. It counseled her to work, for it claimed work was a cure for the pain. She took the article at its word and found her grief pacified. It was the best she could do in her years of grieving.

If you are poor, if you are rich, continue to work.
If you are happy, keep right on working,
        for idleness gives you room for doubts and fears.
If disappointment comes, work.
If sorrow overwhelms you and loved ones seem not true, work.

When faith falters and reason fails, just work.

When dreams are shattered and hope seems dead, work.

Work as if your life is in peril; it really is.

Whatever happens or matters, work.

Work faithfully and work with faith.

Work is the greatest material remedy available.

Work will cure both mental and physical afflictions.

Work sent thoughts of Therese Marie and Len underground. The years were tolerable. "I was determined my children would learn the values I treasured, so I spent my time at home being available for them at all times."

But eventually the nest emptied, and Madeline's thoughts returned to the child she had never seen or touched. As the memories kept recurring, she ached because she had never visited the grave. "I felt an urgency to find it and to name the spot in which she lay. Gradually I acknowledged that thirty-seven years was long enough to ignore her. I hurried to the cemetery office, chose a monument, decided upon the inscription, and paid for it in full. This was the first thing I had ever done without getting the permission of my husband." Len was astonished, but pleased when Madeline invited him to visit the grave.

Then catastrophe struck again. Len collapsed at home and was rushed to the hospital. Thinking that he was fit to go home after some treatment, the hospital released him. The next Tuesday Len gave Madeline a list and asked her to go shopping. While she was gone, he collapsed again and was taken to the hospital. Upon her return Madeline hurried to the hospital, only to find all her children and their friend, Father Paul, gathered around Len's bed.

Len had specifically stated he did not want his life extended by machines. So the family circled the bed holding hands, praying together. Then all present said their good-byes individually and watched until he completed his earthly journey.

"I am at peace," says Madeline, "and am particularly grateful Len and I settled our differences two years earlier. I cried for three days after the funeral, but the emptiness felt good. I feel a calmness and serenity inside that will help me deal with what is in store in the immediate future. I see his death and the way it happened as God's will, and that is enough."

Through the years both Len and Madeline had stored mementos in trunks and boxes. As she went through these, she learned much about Len that she never knew. "Our early years were fairy-tale years, but as time went on, reality set in as our personalities clashed. When I began to realize that the struggle in living out that reality was the real adventure, I began changing. This change helped me to understand who Len was and who I was. So I had no desire to rush through these treasures because I found that even if the slow review of our lives together was painful, it was also healing."

Without healing, we seek
to deaden the throbbing pain.
A poultice is insufficient to treat the wound
until forgiveness and blessing take over.

TIME FOR JOY

Joy is not a feeling such as happiness. We can be happy when we buy a house or attend a concert. These activities, however, do not necessarily bring us joy. Joy is a spiritual energy that is always at work within us. It is anchored in the knowledge that God is present to guide, support, and embrace us in every event and experience. It is an overwhelming appreciation that God is with us and we are in God.

Joy can surface even in pain and crisis. This spirit within us keeps waiting to be called forth. When we set the God within free to relate in love to others, then this time of joy invites a celebration that caresses us in its intensity.

Marilyn, fifteen years old, had been flown in from New York in a coma, suffering from a rare neurological disorder. Carol was a new nurse at the children's hospital in Chicago on the pediatric-neurology unit. She was part of the team assigned to care for Marilyn.

Once treatments began Marilyn regained consciousness for sixteen hours, but relapsed again into a coma. The nursing team, including Carol, worked with Marilyn in twelve-hour shifts for the two weeks she was hospitalized. During her shift Carol took time to see that this fifteen-year-old was groomed and comforted by the touch of another human being. Even though Marilyn was comatose, Carol would often sit with her, trusting Marilyn would sense her silent presence.

The second weekend Marilyn was in the hospital, Carol had a free weekend. Delighting in a colorful dream Sunday night, she was startled with an interruption. In her dream she heard a voice:

"This is Marilyn."

"Oh, Marilyn!"

"I came to say, 'Thank you.'"

"For what?"

"For taking such good care of me."

"Marilyn, I am just doing my job. I am happy to comfort you."

"Carol, I also want to say good-bye and tell you how very happy I am. I want you to feel some of my joy."

Carol was instantaneously enveloped in joy. Marilyn's voice faded as she said, "Again, I thank you."

Monday morning Carol came to work early, eager to check on Marilyn. She went straight to the nurses' station, checking to see who had been assigned to Marilyn on the 7:00 p.m. to 7:00 a.m. shift. The night nurse confirmed that Marilyn had died shortly after midnight.

"Whenever I think of Marilyn's farewell," says Carol, "that intoxicating joy floods my being. That sensation is just as intense as it was when Marilyn said good-bye to me. I know I am in touch with the Divine whenever I experience it."

Joy is an inner quality,
claiming us even when we stand in darkness,
renewing us for tasks ahead.
Joy overwhelms us with the wonder
of the gentle touch of the hand of God,
tendering serenity and peace.

Music persistently dances in Dan's head. When it springs onto the keyboard and is released by the computer, it becomes a song of joy or sadness, a hymn of praise or thanksgiving.

At seven years of age, Dan received his first guitar as a Christmas gift. He taught himself to play the piano while in high school and played trombone in the school band. Although he took lessons, he could also play "by ear." The choir director at his school gave him voice lessons, and he became a member of the boys' choir, singing every Sunday throughout high school. His mentor saw to it that he was steeped in classical music. Later he began playing in night clubs and for commercial recordings.

Composing became urgent and indispensable. His first liturgical piece was the Kyrie, written when he was ten years old. Other compositions soon followed. Rarely did he search for biblical verses or psalms. The music came first and then the words for it.

Eventually Dan became a full-time music director in a parish. He started his musical work by writing responses for the eucharistic celebration. A few years later, Dan composed his first Mass, "Thanks and Praise." Then followed "Living Waters," "Festive Mass," and "Mass in Gospel Style."

After Dan's father died, he composed the "All Saints Mass" in his memory. Dan's father had battled poor health and had come out on top so many times before, that it was numbing for Dan to get the call to go to the hospital. "Dad is dying," was the message. Through the next few days, the family waited, planned the funeral, and reminisced about their father. "For me the funeral was only the beginning of a couple of months of deep thoughts, anger, questioning, and facing my own mortality. I discovered a new appreciation for life, family, and the mystery of creation.

"I still think of Dad, and I am better able to see beyond the pain and loss. I fondly remember a strong, gentle man who loved me enough to teach me how to live. He is physically gone, but lives forever in my siblings and me. The gift he was and is will continue to reveal who I am, and I journey through life with him in memory. Composing that Mass in remembrance was a joy."

Dan focuses on the need for a piece of music, hears the melody dancing in his head, and goes to his keyboard. The Masses he writes are settings fitting the community. His hymns are usually based on his own experiences. While the music comes from his soul, it also expresses the needs of the members of the congregation. Sometimes he picks a thought from the Scriptures and lets the dance begin.

Dan sees the music as a gift from God. "It takes me out of myself and involves me with people. Music is as important a part of my life as eating is. I'm not looking for praise, for composing brings its own satisfaction." Dan is filled with peace, simply bringing joy when he is composing and while working with musicians. His creativity speaks to his soul, and he responds.

The parish art committee commissioned an artist to design a shrine to Saint Odilia, the parish's patron, who had been martyred at an early age. The shrine memorializes the young Saint Odilia on a painting of three panels, filled with young people heading toward the light. One day after the painting had been placed in the entrance to the church, Dan was struck by the light that seemed to be guiding the children. Soon after, during a children's liturgy, the music and the words came to him. He saw these children dancing into the light.

Dan wrote the following hymn in response:

| Am | F , | G | C |

1. One with the saints who have gone be - fore, we be -
2. No long - er lost, we have found our way, we are
3. On - ward we go, we will have no fear, we are

| F C/E | Dm C | Dm7 Dm7/A G |

lieve in the gift of sal - va - tion. *instrumental*
on the path of the sav - ior.
safe in the care of the Mas - ter.

| Am | F | G | Am |

Filled with the won - der of God we are bound for e -
Filled with the Spi - rit of Truth,
Filled with the love of the Lord

| Dm7 | C/E | F6 | Em |

ter - nal life, end - less glo - ry, peace for -

| F | C/E | Dm Dm/A | G | *to Refrain* |

e - ver, with the light of light. We are

With trumpets and the sound of the horn,
acclaim Yahweh.
(Psalm 98:6)

Serve God with gladness!
Come into God's presence with joyful singing!
(Psalm 100:2)

The wilderness and the dry land shall be glad,
the desert shall rejoice and blossom;
like the crocus it shall blossom abundantly,
and rejoice with joy and singing.
(Isaiah 35:1–2)

At only five years old, Tom began to sing and dance. His mother played the piano and loved theater music. At their home in Tacoma, Washington, Tom would sit on the piano bench alongside her and sing the lyrics.

An agent who had seen and heard Tom recruited him for the vaudeville circuit. Songs told a story while dancing provided the emotional and rhythmic response. Tom's circuit included Tacoma, Spokane, and Seattle, Washington, as well as Portland, Medford, and Bend, Oregon. The last swing was through San Francisco and Oakland, California, and then back to Tacoma.

Vaudeville started in the nineteenth century when the Industrial Revolution brought families to large cities. Rules carefully governed the conduct of the performers. No vulgarity was allowed, and performers had to behave politely and professionally. The variety of entertainment included tumblers, acrobats, trapeze artists, fire-eaters, magicians, comedians, tableaus, animal acts, song and dance performers, musical comedy, pop singing, and country and western music.

Vaudeville faded out when the "talkies" were introduced. Tom reminisced, "I remember films like *Naughty Marietta*, with Nelson Eddy and Jeanette MacDonald, as well as *Tarzan and the Apes*, with Johnny Weismueller. When movies became popular, I knew my time on the vaudeville stage was limited."

Out of vaudeville at the age of twelve, Tom began training in solo figure skating and enjoyed the competition, but he did some pair and foursome team skating too. "I remember I had a partner who weighed as much as I did, and when I had to lift her, she barely got off the ground. I started lifting lessons at the YMCA while she took jumping lessons. Soon she was jumping out of my hands. The joy I felt while skating lifted me out of myself, and I felt as free as a bird."

After volunteering for the Army Air Corps in 1944, Tom trained in Texas and Colorado, but the war ended before he could serve. He returned to figure skating. California clubs invited him to perform. "I was so exhilarated, I began ice dancing to jazz music and took the part of a jazz dancer and a shoe-shine man at the only big ski resort and dude ranch at that time in Sun Valley, Idaho."

In 1950, after graduating from Santa Clara University, Tom headed for New York to begin formal study of the soft-shoe dance. This dance was born along the Mississippi River, where Irish vaudeville dancers had encountered black jazz artists from the South and developed the soft-shoe dance. This was a folk-dance art form based on a person's walk, a jazzy, slow four-beat. It was preceded by either a happy or a sad song that reflected what was happening in the country. A grant of five thousand dollars permitted Tom to study this art form in its original state.

By the late fifties, soft-shoe dancing was out, taken over by ballet and jazz. Tom needed a job, and moved to Chicago to learn publishing, then took over as a field editor in Boston. This led him to the executive editor's position with Allyn and Bacon Publishers. As he traveled around the country, he met Joan, his wife. "These publishers accomplished something extraordinary in children's religious-education publications. I organized four of the books in their series and used Jewish art images as illustrations. This was one of my best accomplishments, and I still have copies of these books in my home." Eventually Tom joined the 3M company to write series on health education for schools.

At age sixty Tom returned to soft-shoe dancing. Eddie Sinclair, famous for that art, was willing to coach him in New York, so Tom spent several months under his direction. "I was sixty and Eddie Sinclair was eighty-two when I had my first audition for the soft-shoe technique. He sent me walking Central Park and Broadway's Fifth Avenue for four months. I had to learn how to hold myself properly and stand correctly. Soon I became a standby in off-Broadway plays."

When Theater 65, a theater of and for retirees, opened in Saint Paul, Minnesota, he applied. "I was sure I'd feel like a fool, for I hadn't danced in thirty years. My psyche kept saying, 'You're too fat; you'll fall.' But I got my old orchestrations and took them with me to the local playwright's center where the newly formed theater company was holding auditions.

"I got a job in a play, *Taking My Turn*, about aging in America. I left the business and publishing world and returned to a career that had given me much joy in the past."

Events moved fast. Saint Thomas University in Saint Paul offered office and rehearsal space for the new theater company. Tom became stage manager for *Foxfire*, the second play, followed by the musical *Two by Two*. Once it had a good footing, Tom became the president of Theater 65 and began searching for new space to expand the productions of the seniors.

New avenues opened up for Tom. A high school had its own theater as well as space in the community education office. The school had just inaugurated its drama program, and Tom volunteered to coach the teenagers. "My assistants and I coached outstanding plays. We started with *Seven Brides for Seven Brothers* and went on with *Guys and Dolls, The Man Who Came to Dinner*, and *How to Succeed in Business Without Really Trying*. We also wrote our own play, *Love in the Park*, the anniversary story of Como Park from its beginnings in 1908 to 1998."

In working with older performers, Tom discovered that no one worried about what might go wrong. "I am comfortable and secure in what I am doing because I can draw on my experiences. I'm also doing something I like.

"Another gift is the teenagers, who are fun to work with and eager to learn drama techniques. Even though each year brings a new crop of teens, the reward is great." Tom recalls a German youngster who exuded confidence when he said, "I never knew I could be so good." He was blond and had played a dark-haired Cuban in *Guys and Dolls*.

During the summers, Theater 65 produces plays at an outdoor theater, involving senior actors who invite some of the teenagers from Como Park Senior High School to join them. "Everyone is delighted with this arrangement, the seniors, the kids, their parents, the teachers, and the audience. Young people working with older people is a good combination.

"I demand quality, and the students are aware this requires discipline and perseverance. I feel honored to teach them how to bring joy to others through their performances. This time in my life is bringing closure to the beginning of my musical journey when I was five years old."

David danced before the LORD with all his might.
(2 Samuel 6:14)

Let them praise God's name in a festive dance;
let them sing praise to God with timbrel and harp.
(Psalm 149:3)

Time for Seeking

Our entire life's journey is one of seeking. At times what was habitual, safe, and secure catches us short when we realize that there might be new horizons if we but risk moving toward them. New experiences and discoveries, if sought, may unveil hidden mysteries. We need to sift the chaff from the wheat, open ourselves to God's guiding spirit.

Even when we feel we are getting nowhere, remembering time as God understands it can encourage us to keep seeking. Eventually patience and trust will bring their own rewards, as can be seen in these stories from times of seeking.

Clark Morphew has set himself an important goal of defining various religions for average newspaper readers in order to create in them a respect and tolerance for religions not their own. For over fifteen years, he has averaged two hundred articles a year that are syndicated in two hundred forty newspapers.

A long road preceded this new direction for Clark. His first professional effort was as a teacher in an elementary school in North Hollywood after getting a degree in communications and public speaking from the University of California in San Fernando. However, ministry in the Lutheran church kept tugging at his heart. By his late twenties, he had been ordained and appointed to the Grand Forks United Lutheran Church in the District of North Dakota—a long way from southern California. He became the minister of education, and served for thirty-six months in a conservative, predominantly Norwegian Lutheran congregation.

"My next appointment was as a senior pastor in a blue-collar congregation in Cottage Grove, Minnesota, where for eight years, I developed programs that doubled its size. I also remarried after an earlier divorce, but had to leave the parish because of the negative response by some members to the divorce. It was a painful situation."

After moving to Minneapolis, Clark worked for a publishing company, developing materials for junior and senior high school education. Two years later Clark became a freelance writer for the *Saint Paul Pioneer Press*, and is currently a full-time religion writer for the paper.

Gradually he began moving away from the Lutheran mainstream. "I sensed it wasn't only mainline churches that possessed the truth, and began a calm, reasoned search for a faith that would fit me. I sold all my theological books, even the Bibles, and began a deliberate exploration of world religions.

"I opened myself to all possibilities and so have met the best and the worst of religious leaders. I have also learned I cannot burn my bridges, that I need some of my past connections, for they have been important in my life."

The new possibilities led to a meeting with the Dalai Lama and travel throughout the country. "I make no judgments about any of the religions I study or about the churches I visit. I present my observations and knowledge to the reading public primarily to broaden their horizons and to help them understand that humanity keeps searching for an understanding of God. Not everyone's search leads along the same path.

"I, too, keep searching. God's presence in my life has moved me to openness and to listening to the stories of others. These I want to share with my reading public. Readers are free to accept or reject them. Hopefully, though, they will become tolerant of those whose beliefs are different from theirs."

God, why is it so hard to wait
as we seek to get to know you
in the universe as well as in our hearts?
Time seems empty as it crawls
like a tortoise toward fulfillment.
Inside me churns impatience,
for waiting is empty space
destroying the peace within.

I want things done on my timetable.
Yet, my God, you see the completed picture
while I stare at the tiny pattern before me.
You come in the whisper of a mild breeze
while I demand the dramatic arrival of a whirlwind.
You walk at your own pace
while I hop from here to there,
missing your arrival.
You offer me love,
but I haven't the time to enjoy it.
Twenty centuries ago Jesus touched the earth.
Many knew him not, for they were waiting
for figments of their own imagination.
Calm me, slow me down. I need to wait.
In that waiting, fulfill your time in me.
My welcome mat is out.

Zeita Marie is on a constant search. "I've learned to follow my inner voice, my higher self, finally embarking on the journey toward truth through meditation, for the food needed for soul growth is provided there."

Zeita Marie believes that to find truth, she needs teachers, and they come along when she is ready. "Everything is in divine order. There are periods when learning is achieved in leaps and bounds. At other times one is on a plateau, which allows time for absorbing what has been learned. There are also those periods that are dry times, like the desert, when one does not seem to make any progress."

In Zeita Marie's experience, each person develops at different spiritual levels because of different lessons, if the individuals have not shut down spiritually. "There are those who stagnate from the time they reach adolescence. As they age they are willing to learn new trades, new ways of doing things, new skills, but are quite reticent in developing spiritually."

Because Zeita Marie is a searcher, a teacher gave her a special name, Kamylanthos, meaning "student." Sometimes her teachers call her Master's Savanti, a spiritual student. At other times she is called one of the Spirit's dearest *chilas*, again meaning "student."

Zeita Marie is convinced she has no right to interfere with the will and beliefs of another. She waits until someone crosses her path and begins asking questions, which opens the door to learning for that person. Then she feels free to share. "Spiritual growth cannot be forced. Everything is in divine order and everything happens in God's time, not mine. I have discovered I cannot push the river; it must flow as gently or as rapidly as it will.

"When I am on the spiritual path, I become anxious, because I want to make progress and try to speed it up. I realize I need to relax and let the lessons unfold. It's so simple, but yet so hard."

As life unfolded, I left the place of nesting, of heritage,
to wander through the place of college, marketplace, and shelter,
in the here and there, until I found an anchor.
Needs shifted as my desires turned toward the God of my life.
His cross and Resurrection made me secure.
At last I knew. The place I own within me
is not for sale or rent or giving.
It is in this space stories unfold as I rendezvous with God.
It is here I discover the mirror that reveals myself.
I recognize that in wandering from place to place
as Abraham and Moses and Jesus did,
I should not have permitted any place to demand my strict attention.
This is the place the Creator has made; God's Reign is within me.

TIME FOR TRANSFORMATION

If we live, we will fail at times. Then we wonder what life is all about, why weakness and evil have the upper hand. Succumbing in these instances by our defiance, our denial, blaming others or circumstances only harms us. We can become victims condemned to our emotional cages.

Healing comes when we release pride from our heart and let others and the Other pour balm upon our wounds. Then we can enter a time of transformation.

You're ugly, ugly, ugly!" was the constant refrain she heard in her head. Katie would look into the mirror and see an ugly face. Shy, she withdrew from all play and social activity. The tape in her mind would not let up. Katie was an only child until she was thirteen years old. She believed she was a loser, and she felt guilty about anything and everything. Katie was convinced she was a defective human being, that some vital element was missing in her that kept her from being whole and connecting with people. She knew God found her repugnant too.

Katie never believed that she belonged anywhere, not to a family, neighborhood, church, or community. She would feel sick inside at having to interact with people. She tried to avoid other people. Katie was convinced that she deserved nothing good in life.

Her parents divorced when Katie was three years old, and she was shamed by it. Through elaborate stories she spent her childhood trying to keep the secret that she came from a broken home.

When Katie was nine years old, her father remarried for the third time, and Katie vowed that she would never intrude in his life. Katie never asked nor expected him to be a father to her now that he had another family to love. This withdrawal crushed her because she adored her father and yearned for a close relationship.

Katie was twelve when her mother remarried. Her mother's disastrous second marriage left Katie suspicious of men, sure they could not be trusted to be sexually faithful. Three years later her mother divorced again.

Then one day Katie got a pleasant surprise. She was a teenager. When she looked in the mirror, she saw a young lady who was pretty, and she slowly began to believe it. For three short years, she felt elegant, inside and out, but she still lacked the confidence to delve into her interests. Her looks now let her feel accepted by others, but she never felt acceptable herself. Because she still felt inadequate, she developed the need to look, act, and be perfect, so others would accept her as at least average.

At eighteen years of age, Katie married, but marriage didn't change things. Immediately all the destructive emotions of her childhood returned with fury. The disparity between feeling pretty outside and ugly inside tortured her. Her self-loathing led her to give in to her husband, for he had made it clear that he was the one who knew how to do things correctly. So she submitted to him, accepting the decisions he made, the policies he set. She felt she deserved to be ill-treated.

For the first fifteen years of marriage, Katie was severely depressed, constantly anxious, and persistently ill. Not ever having had a model, she did not know how to give or receive love. She became suspicious and insanely jealous. Her self-loathing destroyed any chance of an intimate relationship.

Eventually Katie sought out a priest to tell him of her emptiness. He recommended that she look into Emotions Anonymous (EA). After checking it out, months passed before she got enough courage to attend a meeting.

During the meetings Katie passed whenever she was invited to talk, but she did listen to the stories of these bruised people. She discovered other people like her, trying to unlock their hearts. She began to say a word or two as her feelings took on a life of their own and begged to be released.

Throughout her life Katie had spent many nights crying herself to sleep. To others she appeared stoic, tough, and defensive, for she never let anyone break through the monumental wall she had built to hide her pain and shame. But once the wall cracked at EA meetings, she stopped crying for herself. Now tears flowed at the sight of a sunset, with an affirming word, in the presence of a smiling child. A friend suggested that she had received the "gift of tears," a power of the Holy Spirit, given to those who are open to mysteries both inside and outside themselves.

Katie still struggles when something overwhelms her, but she turns to her step-by-step program to review again the principles that have led her to freedom. She embraces serenity as she wrestles with the phantoms still trying to destroy her. She recognizes that her walls have tumbled, and is grateful that she was not buried in their rubble. She is determined they will not rise again as she moves on the path of transformation.

To move toward conversion,
to uproot damaging behavior,
to set a new direction
means altering attitudes, seeking guidance.
Grant me the serenity to accept the things I cannot change,
the courage to change the things I can,
and the wisdom to know the difference.

Working on construction away from home for twenty years played havoc with family life. Before Wilson knew it, his wife was dating other men. They were partners, however, in their drinking habits. The stronger of the two, Wilson's wife abused him verbally and emotionally. Wilson was sure that he was worthless.

They had two sons and one daughter whom the mother claimed for herself. Wilson was not allowed to see them. In his dejected condition, he was picked up for driving under the influence. He wondered, "Is it because I am a Navajo that I was sentenced to six-and-a-half years in the penitentiary for a first offense while others simply get a slap on the wrist?"

While Wilson was in prison, he had time to attend college classes. "I also had time to uproot my alcoholic habit through AA counseling, which opened up a new avenue for me, especially in dealing with relationships. I began to believe in myself." His appeal was dismissed, but a compassionate lawyer took over his case, and he was discharged after three years.

"When I was released from prison, I contacted my adult children and was able to establish a healthy relationship with them. They were no longer under the total influence of their mother, and they have begun to respect me. I also refused to do construction work because of the havoc it had done to my life. Having learned a carpenter's trade while in prison, I joined the Carpenters' Union of Arizona. Now I know I can achieve the dreams I have."

Wilson is proud of his heritage. The Navajo is the largest of all the American Indian tribes in the States, with territory the size of West Virginia and a government similar to that of the United States. The tribe has medical facilities, schools, and oil refineries on its land in Arizona. The Navajo helped the United States defeat Japan in World War II. "Our language was not a written one, for it had no alphabet or other symbols. The irony is that when we went to the government schools, we were not allowed to speak Navajo, and yet it is this language that was devised into a code that enabled the Navajo Marines to outwit the Japanese."

These "code talkers," as they became known, and their vital service remained unknown until President Reagan declared 14 August National Code Talkers' Day. Credit is now being given to the anonymous warriors who helped this country win World War II. A monument to these honorable men stands in front of the American Indian Museum in Albuquerque. In his transformation Wilson can now claim this tribal heritage, a family of his own, and his own dignity.

Transformation,
metamorphosis
sometimes require
shock, upheaval,
a radical catalyst
to alter perceptions,
drawing us into health and wholeness.

Joe was told he was dying. He had been diagnosed with lymphosarcoma, and the doctors gave him no more than five years to live. He prepared himself for the inevitable, deciding to withdraw from family and friends so they would not miss him when he was gone.

Joe and Monica, his wife, never talked about this inescapable sentence. He believed Monica had told their five children about his condition, and he was sure they understood why he no longer showed any affection or any interest in their concerns. The separation was gradual. He found excuses to bow out of playing family games, of participating in the children's activities. Independent interests left him in a lonely place.

Monica denied his condition. She wouldn't change his dressings. Joe urged her to consider how she would make a living once he was gone. Monica decided that she wanted to teach dance. Because Joe was up to it, he went with her for lessons in ballroom dancing. Eventually they set up a dance floor in their basement and began advertising that Monica was giving dancing instructions. The response surprised them, and the basement filled with music several times a week.

The treatments burned Joe's skin. Unexpectedly, in a year the cancer was completely gone. He was given a new lease on life. "This healing convinced me that God was calling me to a new vocation. Given this new chance, I decided to dedicate what life I had left to work with 'the least of these,' by helping young people who were in trouble."

Before his illness Joe had taught industrial arts and had served as a coach for football, basketball, baseball, wrestling, and swimming teams in high school. "With the urgency I felt to make the most of the time I had left, I took group-dynamics training and learned intervention skills for AA and drug groups. I applied for and received a grant to experiment in forming a school within a school by separating problem youngsters and giving them the special attention they needed."

He focused on truancy, and insisted the teens take not only regular classes but additional classes as well. Joe's main goal was to prepare them for living. So he convinced local businesses to give them apprentice jobs. The program was such a success that he traveled throughout the country to share the experience.

"But I forgot my own children by ignoring them and focusing on other youths. It didn't dawn on me that they too were 'the least of these.' I began to realize that there was a great rift between them and me." And by now Monica had divorced him.

This separation from his children weighed heavily on Joe. To mend the rupture, Joe started inviting each one individually for a meal. "I explained my motivation for my withdrawal when I was ill and apologized for ignoring them while focusing on other youths. Healing and acceptance have taken time, but my adult children are gradually renewing their relationships with me."

As an industrial-arts teacher, Joe had focused on woodworking. When the parish built its church, he volunteered to construct the furniture. His talent became his legacy, for the church is graced with his hand-built altar, pulpit, tabernacle, and processional cross. An artist designed the sanctuary cross, but Joe did the wood carving.

Joe's experience with death has made death less forbidding. He has planned his funeral service, chosen the hymns he wants sung, and selected significant persons for his eulogy. "I have made a pine coffin with rope handles and filled it with aromatic red cedar inside. I keep it in my living room set against the wall, covered with a decorative runner. I set my crèche and a small tree on it at Christmastime. For most of the year, my television has the spot of honor.

"My thoughts drift to death, but I am not afraid of it. What I do fear, however, is to live too long, to become a burden, or to end up in a nursing home. I will accept death whenever it comes, but I am preparing for it. I don't know the when, but I welcome it enthusiastically. It gives me great freedom, for as I look at my coffin, it reminds me that when I lie within it, I will already have been embraced by God."

Terminal illness—
a blessing or a curse,
depends upon the viewpoint.
Closing down, withdrawing from life
destroy.
Accepting death opens and restores
the assurance that life is worth living.

TIME FOR VICTORY

Few people can claim that they have not felt impotent, blundering, and ineffectual. We struggle. That's part of living. But we determine whether our struggles will lead to defeat or to victory. Will we let God's grace guide us? If so, a time for victory is inevitable, though it may not be in a form we would have chosen.

One of six children raised in a Charleston, South Carolina, Catholic family, Julie Peeples was steeped in the traditions and beliefs of the church. By the end of high school, she was on fire with the desire to be a priest. "I was sure the pope would change his mind by the time I went to the seminary, but the bishop of Charleston forbade me even to discuss it."

So it was not to be. Julie enrolled at Furman University, a Southern Baptist school in Greenville, South Carolina, to major in music and religion. "Something very important happened to me in my religion class. I learned about the Protestant doctrine 'the priesthood of all believers.' That gave me hope, for I could see that all of us are priests, all of us are invited to minister. I was determined to be ordained."

After Furman, Julie enrolled in the Andover Newton Theological School, an American Baptist and United Church of Christ seminary in Newton, Massachusetts. "The experience here supported my desire for the priesthood, and I was particularly impressed with the seminary's vision of Jesus as healer and reconciler. The emphasis on social justice also attracted me."

When she finished at the seminary, Julie found a job as campus minister at a Catholic college in Pennsylvania. Struggling with the Catholic faith and its restrictions, she found another roadblock in one of the priests who constantly abused her verbally. "Because he didn't like the closing hymn I had chosen for the student retreat, he threatened to hurt me. When others heard the shouting and came to help me, I slipped out and later reported him. I also reported him at another time when I discovered he was having sex with students."

The college administration did nothing about either situation, even though they knew about the priest's sexual exploitation. Julie was puzzled. "Why can a priest like that say Mass and I cannot?" The injustice pained her deeply.

Julie exited from the Catholic church. "It was difficult, and I had much soul searching to do. Finally I realized I was not walking away from God, but God was opening up some door in Protestantism through which I needed to walk. It was a significant turning point in my life."

Paul Davis and Julie were married, and one year later, Julie was ministering at the First Congregational United Church of Christ in Winchester, Massachusetts. In June 1988 she was ordained a Congregational minister.

After Julie's ordination, pastors' wives shunned her at a ministers' conference when they learned she was a minister herself. A woman in a PTA group called her "an abomination of the Lord." Julie became aware that prejudice was just as evident among Protestants as it was among Catholics.

Both Julie and Paul were hired as chaplains at the Habitat for Humanity headquarters in Americus, Georgia, where they provided pastoral care for a staff of about three hundred individuals. "We were working with people committed to what they were doing and actively seeking to put their faith into action. It was the most wonderful job anyone could have wished to have."

Later, interviews with staffers surfaced sexual harassment accusations about one of the executives, and when these were reported, he was transferred. However, he returned to his position eventually and fired about forty people as a cost-cutting move. Two of the forty were Julie and Paul. "We were devastated," remembers Julie, "for we knew he had fired us because of our earlier reports. We had hoped this ministry would last many years."

In retrospect Julie acknowledges: "Over and over I can see the good that can come out of wounds, the healing that is possible. I believe God is up to something, but it is not creating calamities. It is that God is right there in them, helping us create good out of them."

Two months after the firing, Julie was in Greensboro, North Carolina, interviewing for a part-time Christian education position in the Congregational church. "I was sure God was up to something. I felt I had come home." She was invited to become the interim minister of the three-hundred-thirty-member church. Soon she became its first female pastor.

Membership had been declining the past four years, but the congregation acknowledged that Rev. Julie Peeples had won them over with her openness, simplicity, and ability to listen without taking sides. "There had been much pain in this congregation. I was struck by the pervasive need for healing, whether it was to address an injustice or to be with someone in crisis. So many times I had needed healing myself, so this made me aware of that need in others.

"There were many misunderstandings among the members, so I encouraged them to talk with one another instead of about one another. My ministry is that point of intersection between my abilities, the needs around me, and what God wants. This is God's dream."

Many changes followed. Members rewrote church bylaws, restructured boards, bought new hymnals using inclusive language, and raised a quarter of a million dollars to renovate the sanctuary. "That was all well and good, but what heartens me is the people's involvement in church activities and retreats." The congregation grew as the word circulated that the minister was a woman who could preach God's word and relate it to people's lives.

Guiding Julie's ministry is the question, What is missing here that I am called by God to make present? "I'm not trying to bring God to people, but I am trying to surface what I know is already there." Her own struggles and setbacks have provided insights she would not have had if everything had run smoothly.

Julie wonders what she can do about the tragedies that envelop people's lives. She asks: "What can I do? Is a prayer vigil sufficient? Should there be something more tangible? How can we make social justice available for all? How can God's dream be made reality?

"God has called me to this time and place. God wasn't asking me to fit into the mold of the traditional minister. God was asking me to minister because of who I am—fears and shortcomings and all. And that is sufficient. That is Christ's victory."

Rev. Julie Peeples has found her niche, the one she dreamt of as she identified with the vision of Jesus as healer and reconciler while studying years before.

What does it mean to struggle?
to feel vulnerable? to feel lost?
What price does one pay for tranquillity
while surmounting pressure and opposition?
Listening to the Spirit
calls us to the right time and place
for the victory of grace.

Convinced that God had guided him throughout his political life, Wayne took some precarious steps when he spoke out against the war in Vietnam. "I cannot recall any time when I was not involved in politics. My father was the county recorder of deeds, and I remember campaigning with him when I was nine." As a conservative Republican, his father disparaged the New Deal and F.D.R.

As a student in high school, Wayne became interested in World War II, and after graduation enlisted in the Navy as a hospital corpsman. "My other interest at the time was the United Nations. I supported the U.N.'s actions in Korea and was on a ship with the Seventh Fleet in the Pacific, supporting opposition to military aggression by North Koreans. I was very disappointed with General MacArthur's actions above the 38th parallel." Wayne went to college, earned his degree, and joined the Democratic Party.

In the late 1960s, Wayne began to publicly criticize U.S. military involvement in Vietnam. "I spent three years in the Navy, from 1948 to 1951, and one thing I defended in the Navy was freedom of speech. Other veterans didn't support my opinion of the war, but I went public. Everybody in our group was a veteran who knew what war was, who had fought for the freedom to talk about it and to take a stand. I couldn't let this opportunity pass me by, even if others decided not to say anything."

Wayne introduced a resolution at a political district meeting in his hometown to withdraw U.S. forces from Vietnam. This was not well received, but it sparked neighborhood organizations to support Eugene McCarthy.

"When the United States became involved in Nicaragua, I feared our country was fomenting terrorism there. I visited the country in February 1987, and my fears were realized." Wayne joined a Veterans' Peace Action team that year to monitor the ceasefire.

After he heard Fr. Roy Bourgeois, a Maryknoll priest, speak about the School of the Americas, Wayne joined the pilgrimage to Fort Benning, Georgia. Wayne was the spokesperson for the delegation to deliver petitions to the commandant to close the School of the Americas. "How could I not speak out?" he asks. "It has been proven that the school has trained terrorists for Latin American countries to torture and kill their poor people."

Wayne organized three groups of Minnesotans who protested at Fort Benning, and he participated twice in vigils on the steps of the Capitol in Washington to draw attention to the school. Wayne has served on ten delegation journeys, including Mexico, Guatemala, El Salvador, and Costa Rica. He joined Father Bourgeois to visit atrocity sites in Central America.

Wayne is convinced of his positions, and feels God has graced him with perseverance in spite of criticism and opposition. He praises Marie, his wife, and his family, who have supported him, even when they didn't always agree with him.

Wayne has many friends who are institutionally bonded to promote justice and peace in church and labor. He joyfully proclaims: "I am proud to be a member of the Veterans for Peace. Even when it was a time for war in our country, I opted for a time for peace, publicly speaking out." In that act of conscience is victory.

Convictions—sources of struggle.
Yet grace-filled determination triumphs over obstacles,
redoubling its endeavors when injustice reigns.

Faith and trust provide the confidence
to march forward for the victory of Christ's peace.

Paul has an allergy to alcohol. One drink leads him to another. Timing, willpower, or situation have no impact. The compulsion puzzled him for years. He tried every way possible to control the drinking: limiting the number of drinks, drinking only on weekends, drinking only when there were guests. All these well-intentioned plans failed miserably. Morning would find him in the shower with a hangover, repeatedly swearing off the stuff for good.

The morning of 3 November 1990 was different. During the night Paul had his first experience with d.t.'s (delirium tremens). Not only was he physically sick, he was frightened. He went to his guilt chamber, the shower, at 6:00 a.m. As he vomited he felt God come and place a hand in his and say: "Paul, you don't have to do this anymore. Ask for my help."

It had never dawned on Paul that he needed God's help to control his addiction. This revelation suddenly made sense. Paul went through a thirty-day treatment program, followed by an AA (Alcoholics Anonymous) meeting, only because his employer demanded it of him. He still didn't acknowledge that he needed the support of AA if he was to remain sober.

At the first meeting, Paul found support and a sense of belonging. He yearned for the peace and joy these people had. AA meetings became a part of his life. It was during this period of sobriety that Paul turned his will and life over to the care of God.

In recovery Paul admitted that his thinking had been off center. What he had believed was normal was, in reality, an abnormality. Through the years alcohol had been his friend, encourager, comforter, confidant, and reward. The death of alcohol in his life took him through a period of grief, confusion, and fear. He agonized over the possible loss of friends, wondered what others would think of him, and questioned whether he would find fun in life without alcohol. His grieving was intense because he wanted the serenity that recovering alcoholics had, but doubted he could achieve it.

On the other hand, sobriety brought glimpses of hope and peace. Paul began to trust and to make true friends. He began to like himself, and he developed a relationship with God, accepting Jesus Christ as his Savior. Now he could hold the hand that had been extended to him in the shower that fateful morning.

Paul recalled his innocent, youthful desire to live a good life. In his early adult years, he had been sidetracked. Now he had come full circle, back to that boy who had loved people and cared for them. Alcohol had not allowed him to mature, but in recovery he was free to grow again. He began to love and care for people again.

Gratefully Paul now sponsors men in the AA program and shares with them the hope that can also be their grace. He also shared his struggle and recovery with his young son. Paul never wanted this part of his life to be a barrier between them.

For years Paul had been at war with himself, battling a compulsion that almost destroyed him. After his victory, peace has come to Paul, and he can enjoy the serenity that is his spiritual inheritance.

God, our higher power, brings
victory, crowning the struggle with success.
We are not alone, isolated
from such amazing grace.

TIME FOR WORK

When individuals worship their work, life shifts out of balance. Family, relationships, and health can fall victim to the consuming desire for power, influence, success, wealth, and acknowledgment. Yet work is an essential part of life, providing satisfaction in tasks well done. Genesis shows the Creator telling humankind to earn its bread by the sweat of its brow, but God also compensated this chastisement by making us cocreators in this universe. We are called to build a better world.

Meaningful work can also be balanced with leisure. The body needs time to recuperate, and the mind and spirit need time to relax. Leisure opens us to discovering and releasing creativity. Leisure unveils new challenges and opportunities to serve God and humanity with love. Leisure allows God to work in us and through us.

Josh went back to college when his collegian daughters challenged him to complete his degree. By studying two nights a week to complete his course work, he graduated six years after his daughters. His degree helped him find a better job with a building and manufacturing company.

In the late 1980s, the company was fighting a takeover, and finally it bought itself out by purchasing all its stock. This plunged the company into debt. It began selling off some of its divisions. By the end of the year, thousands of employees had been laid off. Josh was one of them. "I didn't like the timing because it was before Christmas, but we realized the rationale. If the pink slips had arrived in January, the company would have owed us vacation payments. It was a very unpleasant Christmas gift."

It took Josh six months to find another full-time position with a distribution company more than fifty miles from home. His salary plummeted ten thousand dollars. "It matters not whether it is a takeover attempt or the downsizing of a company, it is always the workers who suffer. The top brass don't take that into consideration. Instead their salaries increase substantially. In addition it is the oldest workers who are laid off first because their salaries are the highest."

Josh's family was living with his mother in a two-flat home in separate apartments. "My mother was from the 'old country,' and emigrated to the United States after World War I. She was highly religious and strong-willed and wished to regulate our lives, threatening God's punishment for our 'sins.'" There were constant verbal battles, and Josh wondered if this might not have affected his wife's health. She has high blood pressure and has undergone open-heart surgery with a quadruple bypass.

After Josh's mother's death, the family moved out of the neighborhood. His oldest sister helped with the down payment on their new home, as she had with college expenses. His daughters, conscious of the debt their parents had incurred, helped financially once they had jobs. "Not only am I grateful but I am comforted, knowing that people who love and care for us show it in so many ways."

In their new home, Josh and his wife entered into a cooperative project. They began gardening, naming their piece of land the English Cottage Garden. "It is not formal in any respect. When we see a plant or flower we like, we plant it, even if the colors clash. We have close to one hundred species here."

His wife, Melanie, has started her own on-and-off business, drying the flowers and framing them, making wreaths and other fantasies. They also welcome animals and birds that find their way into the garden. To manifest their welcome, they put out food and birdseed daily.

The daughters are on their own now, and Josh and Melanie have retired. She does volunteer work in a neighborhood hospital. "We have had some difficult times in our lives, but we have learned much from our experiences. In our final years, we seek peace and tranquillity, and we wish to enjoy together whatever time we have left."

The time in retirement proved short-lived. Josh found out he had lung cancer. Having begun smoking at age thirteen, he had never been able to quit. By the time his cancer was diagnosed, it had invaded his lungs, stomach, and brain. Four months later it was discovered in his pancreas and bone marrow. By this time he was in hospice care at home.

For the last two weeks of Josh's life, his family gathered to be with him. Together they received Holy Communion with him, then blessed him, laid their hands on him, and expressed their farewells. He now had their permission to die. And Josh knew that it would be all right. Sometime in the weeks of his illness, he had dreamed that his Dalmatian, who had died recently, had a flashlight in his mouth and was leading Josh toward a tunnel. Somehow Josh knew that his mother and dad were waiting to welcome him too.

Finally Josh went to meet his Creator. His earthly work was done. Because he had served in Korea, Josh wanted to be buried at Quantico Military Cemetery. At the memorial service, his wife received the American flag in gratitude for his service, his work for the country.

Work,
stimulating activity, purposeful engagement,
capitalizing on talents and skills.
Work,
drudgery by which we eke out an existence,
trapped in abusive situations
that seem to lead nowhere.
Work,
influencing lifestyles,
leading one to wealth or poverty,
inducing surrender to consumerism,
snaring us in debt.
Work,
resource for creativity and meaningful accomplishment,
investing and producing achievements
for the common good.

Laura can trace her interest in political science and government to her junior high school years. These were her electives in high school, and she focused on government in college. She hoped to run for the legislature eventually, but became disillusioned because of the cost of running for office. She turned to law instead.

While preparing for her bar exam, Laura clerked at the federal defender's office, and did one summer's internship and research for three professors. She also clerked for two lawyers, garnering important experience. After passing her bar exams in Illinois and New York, Laura began working for the state attorney of Du Page County, Illinois, in the traffic, misdemeanor, and juvenile divisions.

After marriage and the birth of her first two children, Laura worked as an independent lawyer, then quit entirely during her pregnancy with twins. "It was difficult being inactive all those months, but the twins were born healthy. It also gave me time to evaluate my work." The following year Laura opened her own practice, focusing on family law, which included adoption, guardianship, divorce, child support, neglect, abuse, custody, paternity, runaways, and delinquents.

"Working in these areas has surfaced cynicism in me," Laura says. "I have seen lawyers manipulate the system and parents ignore their children. It is not a pretty sight. Divorce cases in particular are nasty. When one parent derides the other, it damages the child. Chances are that the more acrimonious the divorce, the higher the possibility the children will land in juvenile court."

Laura first attempted to be sure a couple had examined every option before dissolution of the marriage. She used to remind them: "If you hire me, it will cost you one thousand dollars every time we walk through the courthouse doors. The bills will keep climbing, so choose your fight wisely and know you mean it."

In her concern for the children, Laura also advised couples to do long-range planning: "What will be the immediate effects after the divorce? Do you have funds to live on your own? How will this affect the children? The children's needs should be primary, yours secondary." Nevertheless, divorce proceedings became so painful that Laura discontinued her divorce practice. Instead she developed a plan for trial preparation for lawyers that helps spouses mediate their differences rather than litigate them. She recalls one case in particular.

Kathleen had had brain surgery when she was young. After marrying, she adopted Jimmy, a seven-year-old autistic boy who also had an attention deficit disorder (ADD). Because Kathleen had brain problems, both she and Jimmy were on medication. Because she was frequently forgetful, she began recording her phone conversations. When Jimmy began being particularly aggressive, she called the doctor, who told her to increase the medication both for Jimmy and for herself.

Jimmy lost complete control and had to be taken to the hospital. Kathleen grew excessively nervous. The hospital staff accused her of trying to poison Jimmy and herself through an overdose. Denying the accusation, Kathleen pleaded that Jimmy would remain hospitalized until she was well enough to take him home. Instead the Department of Children and Family Services (DCFS) put Jimmy into foster care and into a new school district. This disoriented him even more.

At the same time, Kathleen was going through a traumatic divorce. Her husband used the situation with Jimmy to his advantage and tried to get custody of the boy. After her release from treatment, Kathleen wanted Jimmy to go home with her, but the DCFS refused.

Kathleen came to Laura, who took the case pro bono. The tapes Kathleen had made exonerated her, and Jimmy was returned to her. "I do my homework, for I believe helping the client is primary. It sickens me when lawyers file unnecessary pleadings because someone is just out to make money when the outcome will be the same regardless. It is occasions like this that make me question the viability of my profession."

Laura has halved her working hours so she can be at home when her five children return from school. "The attention I once had is no longer as important to me. Even though satisfied clients refer others to my practice, unless they ask specifically for me and need specialized help, I ask my associates to handle the case. I farm out the work to the staff. All I need to do then is oversee it.

"We delight in money, power, and glory, but I am discovering that none of these can compare to the feeling I have when my children accomplish something and I know I have influenced them. My primary focus now is to guide laws that will support children."

Work
can be a vocation
when its primary purpose is to help others.
Its function, then, is to provide
valuable benefits to those it serves.
Leisure
finds moments in time,
declares holidays when consumed by too much bustle
to recoup dissipated energy.
Leisure
allows creativity to simmer
with ease and contentment,
relaxing body and spirit.
Mingled with labor
it balances the vitality of effort,
equalizing the differences,
leveling the top-heavy, lopsided aspects of life.

D utch remembers the two-room schoolhouse where he first played piano. With his mother as the motivator and his father the financier, he learned guitar and took the Sherwood course in music. This course included piano music of all the great composers. Upon completion of the course, Dutch was expected to write music according to set guidelines.

During grade school and high school, Dutch was the parish organist and choir director of an adult choir in Aurora, Wisconsin. At Saint Norbert's College in De Pere, Wisconsin, he continued his music studies. This gave him a good start when he joined the Air Corps. At Wheeler Field, Oahu, he played in an eighteen-piece dance band and soloed at cocktail parties for the senior officers of the 46th Fighter Squadron.

A few weeks after Pearl Harbor, Dutch's squadron was sent into combat in the South Pacific. "I immediately went to the commanding officer and asked him to ship a piano to Christmas Island, our first stop," Dutch recalls. The captain told Dutch, "If you find a piano, I will be happy to ship it wherever you are assigned."

Dutch borrowed money from a friend, played poker all night, won one hundred dollars, and bought a piano from the chaplain's office at Wheeler Field for fifty dollars. After they shipped out, Captain Sanders kept his word, and the piano arrived within a month. Then within three weeks, the squadron was on the move again. The commanding officer agreed that the piano was good for morale. It followed Dutch to Palmyra, New Hebrides, and then to Guadalcanal.

At Guadalcanal the piano was placed in Dutch's tent on Harmony Hill, where it could be heard by most of the squadron. "It wasn't only our outfit enjoying the music," Dutch says, "but also the infantry and the Marines, who made appointments to come to Harmony Hill." After a year Dutch was transferred back to the States, but first he sold the piano to the First Marines for one hundred dollars.

In Atlantic City the squadron was housed in luxury hotels taken over by the military. Soon Dutch was playing in bars on the boardwalk. That exposure prompted a cocktail bar in Somers Point, New Jersey, to hire Dutch for the summer.

When he got out of the Army, Dutch decided to start over at Lawrence University in Appleton, Wisconsin. His music teacher encouraged him to become a concert pianist. "I tried to meet her expectations by serious practice, but missed being with a dance band playing jazz.

"I turned from concert work and began preparing myself for teaching instrumental and choral music. I continued to play in dance bands on weekends, for I needed the extra money, especially after I married Barbara. Playing the piano for my own and others' enjoyment has been a marvelous gift, an immediate door opener to all kinds of opportunities and experiences."

Barbara met Dutch at Lawrence. Because he directed the parish choir, she joined it. "That was the beginning of our relationship," she says, "and we worked as a team from the very beginning."

As a child Barbara was the best singer in her class. As a high schooler, she sang with a women's chorus that performed in Milwaukee and Chicago. She acknowledges, "Those years were wonderful opportunities for me to learn self-control, and gave me a good sense of my personal grace and gifts."

Once they were married and their children were in school, Dutch and Barbara taught music as a team. She was the music specialist for grades one through five. Dutch taught vocal music in grades six through nine. Barbara also took biweekly singing lessons and sang around town for various occasions. "My knowledge of vocal production helped Dutch's choir work."

"In the early sixties, an event occurred that affected our lives deeply," remembers Dutch. "Saint Joseph's parish, where we worshiped, was not getting enough income to survive. A lawyer friend and I formed a committee to study the situation, and we recognized that survival meant tithing."

Parishioners were asked to contribute 7 percent of their income to the parish and 3 percent to favorite charities. Those making this commitment would not pay tuition for their children through grade school or high school. In addition the parish would pay tuition for boys and girls attending convent or seminary high schools. There would be no more fund-raisers, but there would be parish parties to bring everyone together to celebrate.

Barbara rebelled: "I didn't want to tithe, for I didn't see how we could give away 10 percent and still pay the mortgage and survive. Dutch earned 30 percent less than his public-school counterparts, and I knew we were already contributing much to the parish."

Dutch convinced her. He knew God would provide. "I had no concept of God's love for me," says Barbara, "but I believed in Dutch's wisdom, so I agreed. He would trust the Lord, and I would trust him. This began a journey in understanding that everything is God's and God has given us everything. God loves us unconditionally."

Eventually Dutch became the director of education for the Archdiocese of Saint Paul and Minneapolis. He saw parishes struggling to pay just salaries and to keep their Catholic schools open. "Because Barbara and I had embarked on stewardship as a way of life in the fifties, we were very aware, through the success of our previous parish, that there was an effective way to support church and charity."

At a meeting of chief administrators of education that Dutch and Barbara attended, Msgr. Joseph Champlin spoke about "sacrificial giving," which had been introduced in the Diocese of Syracuse with excellent results. Sacrificial giving used the tithe as a guide for one's gift to the church and to poor people.

Dutch invited Monsignor Champlin to speak about this topic during the Upper Midwest Congress in Minneapolis. Champlin was videotaped, and upon invitation returned with several couples as lay witnesses to encourage tithing. To this workshop Dutch invited several Cursillo couples who also were tithers. Five of these couples enthusiastically agreed to introduce sacrificial giving in their parishes.

Dutch negotiated with the archdiocesan development office to introduce this program, but it was not interested. Dutch and Helen, his secretary, initiated it on their own. The parishes inaugurating the program increased both their offertory and appeal income. But the development office saw this program as an infringement on their work, and Dutch was told to discontinue it.

Dioceses that had seen the Champlin video began inviting Dutch to explain the program to them. "I took over the national leadership, wrote materials, and convinced Monsignor to write an easy-to-follow manual for parishes. I charged a fee for providing materials and training witness couples. The money collected was deposited in the archdiocesan education office budget to offset my secretary's and my time as well as the cost of materials and mailings."

This work had become so important for Dutch and Barbara that when an opportunity to open a stewardship office in the Diocese of Saint Augustine arose, Dutch and Barbara moved there. Here Dutch works full-time developing materials and promoting stewardship in the diocese.

The position requires developing an annual diocesan appeal based on stewardship, establishing a Catholic Foundation, promoting planned giving, and assisting and motivating parish leadership to educate parishioners about stewardship. All parishes in the diocese introduced sacrificial giving and have a renewal annually. Dutch has handed over the national coordination of sacrificial giving to Barbara.

"We are awed at the success of this effort," says Barbara. "During the fifteen years working with Monsignor Champlin, we have produced two videos that are widely used in the United States and Canada. We have personally assisted over five hundred parishes and fifty dioceses in both countries to introduce sacrificial giving and stewardship. We have given witness talks at Masses in over two hundred fifty parishes in this country and in Canada."

Barbara has a number of volunteer presenters around the country that she sends to parishes to give pulpit talks on commitment to sacrificial giving. "It's been quite a ministry these years. It's exciting to be doing it together, for it has brought us into contact with so many remarkable laypeople who truly love the church and want to serve the Lord. Their witness has deepened my faith, helping me accept God's love and protection. God has led us on a special journey!"

Dutch adds: "It was only through prayer and trust that we began tithing over thirty-five years ago. For years both of us have prayed together every day, using the Mass readings of the day with a commentary. Then we pray aloud, sharing what we feel God is inviting us to do that day. This practice has been a wonderful gift to our marriage, and we have found sacrificial giving so fulfilling, we encourage others to experience it too. This is a task we feel we are presently privileged to do, to become evangelizers in parish after parish."

"As volunteers we travel to wherever we are invited, 'plant seeds,' and leave town," Barbara adds. "We pray every day for the parishes and dioceses we have assisted, and we fast the first Friday of each month. This work has made us a part of the mystical Body of Christ. The church is alive and well, and we rejoice about that after serving it in some fashion or the other for close to fifty years."

For surely I know the plans I have for you,
says the LORD,
plans for your welfare and not for harm,
to give you a future with hope.
(Jeremiah 29:11)

TIME FOR MEMORIES

Memories are recollections and memorials to what has happened in our life. When we relive them in bits and pieces, we discover they are chronicles of the heart. The collections stored in our mind-diaries may carry blessings, helping us to recognize that even hurtful experiences are opportunities for growth. Other memories need healing if we are to enjoy life in its fullness. The care of a professional, the support of friends and loved ones, the surrender of the pain to God—all can help us heal our time for memories.

Bill's youngest daughter was leaving for college in New York. Her sister had left two years ago for college in California. As the scene was repeated a second time, Bill struggled with his feelings about letting go. The tears settled in his throat in this repeat performance as he and his daughter shared heart-wrenching good-byes.

He remembered the panic of years ago when his daughters were ages six and four. Bill had taken them to the airport to meet their mother, who was coming home from a vacation in Ireland. He couldn't find the flight listed on the board, so he cautioned his daughters to stand there while he checked things out at the counter. When he returned they were gone.

Panic mobilized him as he started his search in the immediate area. They were not there. He went to the counters, then raced through each concourse calling their names. He could not find them. Two hours later Bill returned to his starting point. Behind the ticket counter he could see the top of his older daughter's head. Next to her was a security officer.

"What took you so long to find us, Daddy?" she asked. "We have been paging you for a long time." In his panic Bill thought only about finding his two little ones; he had not heard his name called.

The memory was vivid, one he would never forget. Now he stood in front of his daughter, temporarily mesmerized, as she waited patiently to say her final farewells before takeoff. The farewell was wrenching. He realized and accepted the certainty that his daughters were both young women stepping into adulthood, preparing for their own destinies. He would need to live on the periphery of their lives. He could put no obstacles in their way. His role now was to pray for, support, and love both of them across thousands of miles.

Memories of what had been,
years of guiding, supporting, loving
seem to fade away in the mist of tomorrow,
wrenching good-byes.
As new opportunities appear on the horizon,
farewells are the order of the day.
Love becomes
letting go.

The year was 1917. Ludwina leafed through the Orphan Train catalog, looking for a boy and a girl that she could order. Blond hair and brown eyes were the requirements. Finally she saw the girl. The child couldn't have been more than two years old, but her wistful smile touched Ludwina's heart. Here was the daughter she wanted.

She kept looking for a boy near that age who would become her son. As she flipped the pages, he leaped out at her. It did not take long for her to make the arrangements. Both children would arrive on the Orphan Train from New York.

From 1865 to 1929, close to two hundred fifty thousand children were placed on orphan trains. Not all were ordered. Many were simply put on the trains heading west, shuttled through towns. This all happened because from the middle of the nineteenth century, the European poor had flooded the United States, moving into a different kind of poverty. That left thousands of children homeless.

Recognizing these outrageous conditions, Charles Brace, a minister and a millionaire, talked some of his moneyed friends into helping these abandoned children. He bought a building in New York City and named it the Children's Aid Society, where deserted youngsters could find a haven.

Babies were abandoned on doorsteps, at parks, in churches, and on convent steps. The Sisters of Charity decided they could not let this go on. They located an abandoned building, begged for cribs, babies' clothing, and medicine, and established Saint Joseph's Foundling Home.

Overwhelmed by the numbers, Brace suggested farming out children to the Midwest. Posters were placed in midwestern towns, advertising the arrival of the children in each town. They followed a simple pattern:

WANTED

HOMES FOR CHILDREN

A company of homeless children will arrive (date).

These children are of various ages and of both sexes, having been thrown friendless upon the world. They come under the auspices of the Children's Aid Society of New York. They are well-disciplined, having come from various orphanages. The citizens of this community are asked to assist the agent in finding good homes for them. Persons taking these children must be recommended by the local committee. They must treat the children in every way as a member of the family, sending them to school, church, Sabbath school, and properly clothe them until they are seventeen years old.

As the train stopped at designated stations, the children were lined up, and adults examined their teeth, felt their muscles, studied their strength, and made their choice.

Some children were virtually enslaved, beaten and abused. Frequently siblings among the orphans were separated and never saw one another again. Although some children were adopted, most of them were only indentured, so that they could be sent back to New York if they did not satisfy the family. Some children were not allowed to go to school because they were needed for farm labor, and so they grew up illiterate.

Mary was but two years old when she was put on the orphan train. A Czech family named Bezdicek, from Jackson, Minnesota, claimed her and the five-year-old Edward of the blue eyes and brown hair. Mary and Edward became brother and sister. They were fortunate because they were wanted and loved. Both grew up as Catholics, because this was the family's faith. However, the parents did not adopt the children. Instead the parish priest signed the indenture papers.

Mary was seven when the children at her Catholic school began making fun of her because she was "adopted." When she asked her mother what adoption was, her mother burst out crying. Not knowing what it was all about, Mary hugged her mother, comforting her with, "I love you very much." The matter was never spoken of again.

Soon after, her parents moved to Saint Paul, where Mary completed her education in public schools. Her mother died when Mary was thirteen, and her father did his best to raise two teenagers. He remarried, and as soon as the children finished high school, Mary and Edward were on their own.

Mary remembers these years as painful ones. "They were rough not because I was an orphan but because I was so lonely. I found it hard to make it on my own, so I moved in with a family in Minneapolis."

Up to this time she had been using the surname Bezdicek. During the war, when she applied for work at Honeywell, social security had already been inaugurated. When she presented her baptismal certificate, the name on it was Mary Sullivan. Because she had never been adopted, she now had to return to using her biological mother's name. "Even though my father didn't like it, I could no longer be a Bezdicek; I was now a Sullivan."

Mary had never met her nineteen-year-old birth mother or her birth father. Neither was she aware that the boy who lived in their household was not her blood brother. However, it really didn't matter; they had grown up as siblings who loved each other.

The revelation about her parents came years later. She needed a passport for traveling abroad. All she had was her baptismal certificate with her birth mother's name, but the passport office did not accept it. In desperation she asked her congressman for help. She had the certificate in a week. She had known her Irish mother's name because it was on the baptismal certificate issued one day after her birth. The blurred name of the father turned out to be Alex Kalman, who was thirty at the time.

Years passed. Mary married and raised her own family. When her husband died and her two children had established themselves, Mary retired to Arizona. "After I discovered that there was an organization for Orphan Train riders, I began attending their annual reunions. There aren't too many of us originals alive today, but we have established contacts with their siblings and children."

When the play *The Orphan Train* was produced in Saint Paul, Mary attended and told her story to the audience. "I don't know what my life would have been like if I had not been 'ordered' by the Bezdiceks. I am grateful for their compassionate and loving care, and hold no resentment for the parents who abandoned me. I have had a rich and fulfilling life, and God has been gracious to me. I do not miss what might have been."

Early memories grow dim,
locked in the chest of yesterday.
Opening that chest, like Pandora's box,
provides no guarantee about what will emerge.
Hindsight acknowledges the years
can be a mixture of kindness and hardship
as new adventures influence the road to maturity,
leading hopefully to gratitude for all that has been.

On the anniversary of Suzanna's death, Anne, her daughter, stood at her grave, overwhelmed by the legacy her mother had left behind when she died from cancer at the age of eighty-seven. Suzanna had come to Ellis Island as a stranger from a foreign land at the end of World War I. Eventually she settled in Chicago, where she married. Anne was one of the three children Suzanna bore.

Suzanna had been a peasant girl tending sheep at the beginning of the twentieth century. Her father did not believe girls needed an education, so Suzanna was taught by her maiden aunt, Rosalia. Years later her daughters taught her more of the fundamentals when they were going to school. She was a fast learner.

Anne remembers her mother as she came home daily from the casing factory. "Mom would have bloody cuts on her fingers where the salt had eaten through. Her feet were frequently swollen as she stood in water in her rubber boots. It was the Depression, and she needed to work if the family was to survive.

"I would watch her in the evenings as she knitted sweaters for sale and designed our clothes. In the summer we had fun picking dandelions in the prairie across from our house and delighted in watching Mom make dandelion wine."

Anne didn't linger too long in the cemetery, but her memory continued reliving parts of her mother's life, so intermeshed with her own. Suzanna never lost the simple Catholic faith in which she had been raised. For her, devotion to the Virgin Mary was important, and she hosted the Fatima statue whenever it made its rounds in the neighborhood. "She considered it important to pray for the conversion of Russia, but she was no longer around when the Soviet Union dissolved."

Suzanna never missed the May or October devotions in the parish, and she saw to it that her children also attended. She joined Mary's Blue Army, whose goal was to pray for the conversion of sinners. She also made scapulars that she distributed lavishly. She honored the last words of Jesus on the cross and promoted that devotion whenever she could. Decades later her oldest daughter authored a book on these last seven cries of Jesus.

Saint Anthony also had his special role. He had to find the things she lost. She had the family consecrated to the Sacred Heart of Jesus, and the framed certificate of that event was kept in a place of honor in the living room.

Although Suzanna missed her daughters, she rejoiced when both entered the convent. "It was hard," says Anne, "because of the strict rules. The family could visit only several times a year, but for Mom it didn't matter. She knew we would be doing the Lord's work in special ways. She had wanted a religious vocation for herself, but knew it couldn't happen because she lacked an education."

Suzanna's son went away to college after the girls entered the convent. The nest was empty. Then the Korean War interrupted her son's college. He was drafted. "Mom had ordered him to study shorthand and typing while in high school in spite of his objections. In Korea he was never sent to the front because he was needed behind the lines as a secretary for the medical corps. Because he never fought, he was spared the nightmares other soldiers suffered. I know he was grateful she had insisted."

Suzanna had no trouble with the changes of Vatican II. She had moved out of her ethnic parish and quickly learned the English Mass responses, joined in the singing, and stayed with the women after Mass to pray the rosary. She loved reciting the Our Father out loud and exchanging the handshake of peace during Mass.

On the way to church one Sunday morning, she was attacked and injured by several men who stole her purse. Anne recalls how fearful Suzanna was of walking the streets alone after that. Even so, she went to daily Mass until she was eighty-three. "When she developed breast cancer and had a radical mastectomy and was too ill to go to church, I began bringing her the Eucharist," says Anne. "Mom kept expressing her gratitude that Vatican II had granted that privilege. She had never dreamed she would have her daughter bringing her Holy Communion in her own home. She saw this as a tremendous blessing."

Suzanna refused radiation treatments, but believed in aggressive vitamin therapy. "Mom lived four more years before the cancer metastasized. She did not want to go to the hospital to die, so we honored her request. I'm glad all of us were there when she died.

"What was hard to deal with was Mom's fear that God might not forgive her. I remember the day when I brought her the Eucharist and she tearfully asked me, 'How can God forgive me? How can God love me when I have been such a sinner?' She wondered if there was an afterlife and if she would be saved. I comforted her, reminding her of the many saints who had gone through similar dark nights of the soul. It was then that she was at peace and waited with anticipation to meet the God whom she had served so faithfully."

Before she died Suzanna made an ethical will, putting her last spiritual testament on tape for her extended family. Her voice was strong as she said, "I want to let you know I love you very much, and so I ask you not to forget me, especially in your prayers. Pray the Lord would be merciful to me, not as a just God but as a compassionate one, for I have offended him many times. God has always forgiven me and loved me, so I believe I will be allowed a happy death, united with God forever.

"My desire and request is that you would love the Lord always until death and would love one another. In this way you will fulfill God's will on earth and be united with God in heaven for all eternity.

"Once more I tell you how much I love you. I beg God to bless you always. I bequeath my love to you until we meet in heaven."

Anne's older sister read this testimony at the funeral Mass. She responded to her mom's request in the name of her children. "We accept this testimony as your final gift to us and know you no longer want to be bound to earth, for that would tarnish your joy. We acknowledge the end of your physical life and the beginning of your eternal life. Be with God, Mom, and enjoy your happiness."

When Suzanna's husband died, she had a monument erected over both of their graves. On it she had engraved, "Jesus, Mary, I love you. Save souls." "She made public what her life had been about," affirms Anne. "Being buried on 18 July 1980, on the fifteenth anniversary of Dad's death, probably was not a coincidence. She was once more united with the man she had loved so much."

Memories are etchings preserved in time,
yielding their secrets now and then
as special moments invite their appearance.
They can be awesome in remembrance.
Even when shrouded by the passage of the seasons,
they can heal desolate hearts
when their recognition is a souvenir
of time spent in precious relationship.

Time for Eldering

Elders are persons who keep growing spiritually and emotionally, and who acknowledge the promise and potential that is still theirs to claim. While embracing the past, they set a pattern for the future, even as they prepare for their own departure.

As the years accumulate, we find that we need to own all that has been, as life continuously shapes us into the persons God has created us to become. Through failures and successes, suffering and joy, illness and health, forgiving and being forgiven, we mature into elders who understand the growth pains of becoming sages.

Each life has worth and leaves a legacy. We will leave a gap for all eternity if we ignore our role to achieve wisdom. Abraham and Sarah left a legacy that spans centuries. Jesus' legacy has changed the world in immeasurable ways, connecting humankind to the Creator and challenging individuals to live lives of love.

By learning from our experiences and sharing our insights with others, we become sages who connect what has been with what will be. Elders can initiate a ripple in life's living waters that extends itself until it is absorbed by other ripples to become one with the universe.

Sr. Angelita Fenker calls herself a "Gospel woman" because she serves God's people full-time. "I love having such a broad-based contact with God's people, from whom I learn so much. It's a joy knowing I've touched the future in a meaningful way, sharing Christ's friendship with others who can carry it on far beyond what I alone might do."

Sometimes her call is lonely. "I can't always articulate my vision so others can understand and receive it. However, this friction is creative, like the friction in a motor, so I accept it."

Angelita was born in Fort Wayne, Indiana, the oldest of seven children. She is currently caring for her mother, who was born in 1899. "It is from her I learned much about growing older." She belongs to a post-Vatican community of sisters who call themselves Sisters for Christian Community (SFCC). Each woman chooses where she will live and how she will work. None wear a traditional religious habit, partly because their goal is to be leaven in the workplace. They do not have a central headquarters or a major superior. Promises are made to follow the guidelines, and the sisters meet annually to review their goals and to deepen community.

Angelita's has been a colorful life. She has been a teacher, a principal, and a director of religious education. She has worked with Father Peyton as the associate director of Families for Prayer and has assisted in research and writing for a parish renewal program used by more than two million families. She earned her doctorate in spirituality from the Graduate Theological Foundation. Angelita has conducted workshops and seminars on family-related topics for clergy, parish leaders, educators, and family groups. She has also worked with teens, the elderly, and military personnel throughout the United States and Canada.

This background and experience have deepened Angelita's belief that age has little to do with the legacy each person must leave upon death. "I see eldering as indicating that wisdom has been accrued through growth, lifelong learning, and mentoring. We can and we must prepare for our eldering process. Becoming a saging-elder and an eldering-sage means lots of challenging, personal work, but work that is extremely rewarding and fruitful for the church and the world."

Angelita claims that the spirit within each of us at the end of life is as young as it was at the beginning of it. The process of living, though, has provided opportunities to mature that spirit. This maturation is what makes individuals wise and puts them in the position of mentoring others. She suggests that what is needed is the intention and attention to develop this spirit, and outlines the tasks required for this development. Chief among these are the following:

• providing a hollow and empty sacred space within the self so God can touch and fill this deepest part of one's being
• responding in new ways to God's "I love you"
• becoming aware of how much love one still has to give

- making sense of the failures and successes in life
- sharing this wisdom with others
- accepting both one's own and others' limitations

"Eldering time provides opportunities to become disciples and stewards to pass on God's message of love. It also allows God to touch us so we can touch others in a like manner." Angelita is convinced that the various stages of life complement and support one another, for this is how individuals remain alive, active, radiant, and vibrant as they enter the crowning stage.

"As with any major step in life, we need God and a deepening participation in God's life and love. This stage in our life is a contemplative time that, when relished, allows God's dynamic life, light, and love to fill our emptiness so we might give our loving selves to a pained and desperate world.

"This time also allows us to understand prayer in a different way. Jesus said, 'Pray always.' He did not say, 'Say prayers always.' Prayer is simply a way of being, of becoming a conduit from God to others. It relates to the sacred space within. Prayer is also accepting the experiences in life in order to learn from them. Prayer is now more easily the opportunity to meditate, to reflect in quiet, to get in touch with the spirit of God as well as with the spirit within."

The Shoshone Indian belief that we need to leave a legacy down to the seventh generation touched Angelita. "It is not enough to will money or possessions to the first and second generations, as we normally do. We need to leave behind the day-to-day, year-to-year, and generation-to-generation family history." This can be done, Angelita believes, by reporting the rituals, traditions, and stories of extended family members.

"By focusing on a generation we will never know, it is much easier to discriminate what is important and valuable. This chronicling can be recorded through a journal or by electronic means. Videos, audios, and camcorders are available for anyone desiring to use them. Photos with captions, personal letters, sacramental certificates, and awards are also useful." The inclusion of accounts of political or historical events can help too. Highlighting the dreams of family members and sharing incidents that have influenced family life, such as religious conversions, births, deaths, celebrations, and education, are equally important.

"With positive attitudes, a great amount of enthusiasm, and cheerful trust in the God who calls and anoints us to share our life's wisdom and experience with future generations, we walk in our eldering-belovedness to take God's dynamic life and love to a world that desperately needs it. This becomes our final gift."

Aging—the opportunity
to become wisdom keepers
for upcoming generations,
leaving a legacy
to inspire and guide those who follow
makes elders into sages.

In Africa every village has a Queen Mother. She is an elder whose heart embraces all in need. She is the trusted confidant to those with problems, for she is wise. The Queen Mother is beloved by the villagers. Frogtown, Minnesota, claims its own Queen Mother.

In 1959 Mary Fletcher came north from Louisiana and Texas with two small children after she left an abusive husband. Mary bore two more children during a second marriage that also broke up. She worked in a laundry for six years and then at the Wilder Child Guidance Clinic in Saint Paul. While at Wilder she learned about an opening as a part-time clerk at a grocery store in Frogtown, the inner-city neighborhood in which she lived.

She worked at the store for a year, taking over more and more of the proprietor's jobs, becoming familiar with the buying and selling. Eventually the owner offered to sell the store to Mary, but having no collateral, she questioned how she could manage payments. The break came when she made special arrangements, allowing part of her monthly salary to become the down payment. Later she was able to secure an adequate loan from the Small Business Administration.

Mary quickly earned a reputation for being trustworthy and for being the heart of the neighborhood. Her heart was open to the poor of the area, and she made concessions for them when needed. She gave children tender, loving care when they came into the store. Soon they were calling her "Mama." When she found a vagrant in the basement, she fed him. The store became a haven for those with problems, and Mary always listened.

Drug peddling, prostitution, assault, and robbery were prevalent in Frogtown in the sixties and seventies, but they did not threaten Mary. In twenty-eight years she was robbed only twice, and the store was broken into once. "The kids used to hang out around here, but they weren't really dangerous. I simply made friends with them. I told them this store is like my home. I wouldn't let you come into my house and run over me, and I'm not going to let you do it here." She earned their respect. The word went around, "Don't touch Mary Fletcher."

Once in the sixties, a man came in and loaded up with meat from the freezer. As he attempted to leave, Mary wrestled him to the floor and locked him in. Some of the kids heard the noise and came to help her. A few days later, the man returned to apologize.

Although Mary was a Methodist while in Texas, she joined the Catholic community in her neighborhood. "I don't care too much for formal prayer, but I pray spontaneously during the day. I am convinced God's strength and grace have been my blessing."

Mary has retired and has set new goals. "I have been called to love, and I intend to use that power to work with children as a volunteer." She senses her reputation as Queen Mother will help her in her new vocation.

Eldering is not a passive task.
It requires working with God
to send the message of love
deeded to humanity by God's only Son.
This graced part of life
is the pearl of great price,
the fruition of the seed of goodness and love—
the eldering time for wisdom-sharing.

He sounds like a robot talking. James holds an artificial larynx along the left side of his neck whenever he speaks. This is his way of communicating now that he has lost his larynx to cancer.

James was just nine years old, selling newspapers on the street, when he began picking up butts. He continued smoking, and this led to an unsuccessful surgery. The second operation seven months later put a hole in his neck, a constant reminder of his folly. He threw away his cigarettes and never smoked again.

James was hard to live with after his surgeries, for the pain and drugs irritated him considerably. He missed working—having been chef at luxury hotels in New York, Philadelphia, and Phoenix. Now when he answers the phone, people hang up on him. Acceptance has grown slowly for James.

"When I look back on my life, I am grateful I am alive. On my seventeenth birthday, I accepted the Lord, who has been close to me since then. I believe I have survived because God still has a task for me to do. I know I have a mission. It seems I had to uproot a damaging habit in order to be ready for it."

Now that James appreciates the life he almost lost, he has discovered his mission. James supports people who have had larynectomies, offering them hope for their own survival.

Understanding
may be the best and only fruit of catastrophe.
In life's last performance,
insight may lead to appreciation
of the time
of eldering;
by acknowledging the foolish,
the painful is transformed into wisdom.

TIME FOR WISDOM

Sometimes we need to stop at road signs to figure out if we are going in the direction we wish to go. At times the road we are on is so enticing or comfortable that it delays us and may even detour us. Then we may need a Damascus experience, one so traumatic and powerful that it rattles us enough to take another route.

Or, we may heed the whispers within us from Wisdom that suggest other directions. The understanding Wisdom offers can penetrate our self-sufficiency and lead us to the surrender that invites God's guidance and protection.

As an entrepreneur, Janie specialized in helping people who were doing shift work. Nothing in her undergraduate work had addressed their issues or prepared Janie directly for this type of work, but her own experience as a teenager doing shift work packing cans of Spam helped her relate to the upside-down life of working nights and sleeping days.

As a county extension educator, Janie had conducted an assessment with a large population that worked shifts at a paper mill, the local utility, and a hospital. The lifestyles these people led and their stoic manner of coping fascinated her. Janie began research on shift work, and spent hours in the university library and at the U.S. Bureau of Mines Resources.

After eighteen months of interviewing and developing a curriculum, Janie taught her first class on "Quality of Life for Shift Workers." Over ninety people came to that session, and she knew she had found her mission.

Janie resigned from the university to devote her full energy to the expected requests for the course, but for a year the requests did not come. She had to collect unemployment. However, she did not remain inactive. Her chief marketing efforts included reading the Sunday papers to circle all the ads for shift workers. She would then call each company to sell her services. Sometimes these cold calls were ignored, but Janie would put their names into a file folder and contact the companies again in a month. Several major contracts developed.

Janie also joined professional groups, and during introductions or round-table discussions, she would let people know about what she was doing. This strategy also brought in some business.

Even so Janie was still having cash-flow problems. In fact, she was nearly bankrupt. For three weeks she had been crying daily, and this day in May was no different. Suddenly she heard a clear voice saying, "Janie, I want all of you." Startled, she paid attention and heard the voice again, "Janie, I want all of you."

Janie responded, "Are you referring to the seventh AA step that says, 'I humbly ask you to remove all my defects of character,' and the prayer that follows, 'I am now ready that you should have all of me, both the good and the bad'?"

The voice just repeated, "Janie, I want all of you."

"Okay, you've got me. I thought you already had all of me, but now you do."

As Janie relaxed in her chair, another AA slogan came to mind. "Do what is in front of you." Janie cleared off her desk, leaned back in her chair, and said, "There's nothing else for me to do but breathe." It occurred to her that breath also meant spirit. As she breathed she experienced this spirit, one second at a time. Soon she felt a different sense of purpose, even though her business seemed to be collapsing.

A few days after Janie had had her talk with God, Disneyland called with a major contract requiring an immediate response. Next, a company from Wisconsin requested training within two weeks. Finally, an insurance company wanted to finalize plans for development of a training manual. In each instance Janie asked for half of the payment up front. She was then able to pay off the majority of her debts.

"The seventh prayer in AA has become a mantra for me. I frequently say, 'My God, you have all of me.' I see I may have been arm wrestling with God and didn't know it." She is grateful for the wake-up call. "I am living on a cliff, never knowing what lies ahead. I guess I'm a cliff-dweller and am learning to trust.

"God is my life. As I recognize my gifts, I acknowledge that I am using them to present alternatives for positive lifestyle adjustments and I know this is God's will for me at the present time. I see myself as 'Janie of Arc,' leading shift workers out of the darkness and into the light. When I am slack in letting God's will be done in me, God reminds me that God is the source of all goodness and I am not all-powerful. It is then I affirm 'You have all of me.'"

God is the light shining in darkness,
dazzling us with luminous wisdom,
granting us the energy to reflect radiance of the Holy One.

Sonny had always felt insecure, unloved, shamed, and inadequate. Being constantly belittled by his father added to his longing for love and respect. To temper the pain, he developed a fantasy world in which he could change his parents, his name, his childhood, and the situations in which he found himself.

By the time he was thirteen years old, Sonny had discovered that alcohol eased his pain. His feelings of insecurity, discomfort, and unease subsided whenever he raided the liquor cabinet at home. His dreams also fueled his fantasy as he imagined himself popular, successful, wealthy, and powerful. "Even when I had a hangover or kept throwing up, I never considered it a problem. My fantasy helped."

By the time Sonny was a junior in college, he was into pot, speed, uppers, downers, and psychedelic drugs, along with alcohol. Life revolved around drugs and sex. "My last semester in college was a disaster. Up to then I had gotten by, managing to get C's in my courses. During this semester my only interests were girls and drugs. I cut most of my classes, and when it came time for finals, I then purchased the books I needed, got notes from my friends, and crammed for days, staying awake with speed.

"I passed the classes, but had a nervous breakdown, constantly crying and wringing my hands. The doctor gave me tranquilizers so I could sleep, but one of my girlfriends stole them. I was a wreck."

The downward spiral continued when Sonny married Sally, his roommate's girlfriend, even though he didn't like her. He felt guilty about having sex with his friend's girlfriend. So to relieve his roommate's anger, Sonny convinced him that he loved Sally. After the wedding they traveled to the Greek islands.

The marriage failed within six months. So Sally, a flight attendant, gave Sonny a ticket to Europe. By sending him off, she could claim desertion.

Somehow finishing college, Sonny picked up a degree and a cocaine addiction. He tended bar, cooked in restaurants, and managed a series of low-paying jobs. None lasted long because of his drug and alcohol abuse. "By the time I was thirty, I was in debt and had no friends. Feeling sorry for myself, I turned to dealing drugs."

One day in Chicago's Lincoln Park, Sonny was taking LSD when he looked up and saw a photo shoot. The young woman was slim and beautiful, eager to show off her body in various poses. Nearby an older woman with swollen ankles was unraveling a dirty bandage from her face. He shuddered as he saw the hole that was her nose.

"I don't really know what happened, but a feeling of despair settled over me. Comparing these extreme images, I desired to know what life was all about. I felt so empty, so disturbed, I decided on suicide. I called Sally, who invited me to her apartment to talk about it. She listened, suggested we have a bath together, then urged me to nap until the morning before killing myself. By then my despair had passed."

Surviving into his mid-thirties, Sonny began flying lessons in Florida, preparing himself to smuggle marijuana from Jamaica. With a former girlfriend, he drove to Key West, where the drug trade was booming. Sonny felt comfortable because he did not stand out. "I discovered laxity there because the police and city officials were into drugs themselves. Their eyes were closed to what any of us did. Soon I was delivering marijuana to Chicago, Minneapolis, North Carolina, the eastern seaboard, and parts of the Midwest. The smuggling went on from the late seventies to 1990."

Sonny used his sailboat to make the rounds from Florida to the Bahamas, Jamaica, and Mexico to pick up drugs. But what had started out as a simple smuggling operation was now becoming violent. "Greed took over, and the dealers began ripping off one another. Even

though I had thousands of dollars of debt, I could not employ violence to get the money. Dealers armed themselves, and I was robbed
of eighty-five thousand dollars and nearly lost my life. Some of my
friends were killed while smuggling. I crashed my plane in Belize. Pi-
rates attacked my boat in the Bahamas." Sonny was frightened.

Despite the violence, for over two months, Sonny sailed his usual route. Most of the time he was drunk. He fell off his boat and kept
brawling with his crew. "My return found me profoundly unhappy. I
was no longer getting a kick out of smuggling, and saw it as a fruition
of my fantasy life. I had money, I didn't need to work, I could control
people, I was as powerful as I had dreamed of being, and I believed I
was successful. As I walked the streets, some people would step aside
as if I were a mad dog. Others considered me a colorful character.

"I began getting true glimpses of myself as the drug addict I was.
My liver hurt, my heart was enlarged, and I couldn't sleep because I
was drinking around the clock. The doctor told me I had about a year
to live. Three of my acquaintances had committed suicide, and that
shook me up."

Amy, his wife of ten years, was also an alcoholic. When Sonny
was out of control, she invited Tom, a recovering addict, to visit them.
Tom told Sonny things he didn't want to hear. "You are intelligent and
talented, but you are wasting your life. I don't want you anywhere
near my family."

Sonny finally admitted that he had wasted his life and that his
fantasy of the early years was not working. He and Amy had tried to
stop drinking several times, but they were never successful. This time,
however, they decided to go to an AA meeting. "I was trembling; my
knees were shaking as we faced about thirty people in that room. I
looked at beat-up faces that were happy and asked myself, 'If AA
worked for them, then why can't it work for me?' It was a real struggle as I worked the steps. 'One day at a time' was the refrain that got
me through. I never drank again."

Sonny looked for a home in Mexico, away from the drug scene.
But friends alerted him to the surveillance by the Drug Enforcement
Agency (DEA). Some other smugglers had reported him. Nine months
after he had started AA, he was arrested for conspiracy to smuggle
eight thousand pounds of marijuana into North Carolina. Even though

the crime was four years old, Sonny was extradited to Virginia to stand trial.

"I pled guilty and reached a plea agreement. My home and all my assets were forfeited, and the government agreed not to prosecute other criminal acts I had committed up to the time of the arrest. What worked in my favor was the fact that I had never been violent and had refused to smuggle cocaine. What also helped me were the nine months of sobriety I had achieved before my arrest.

"I was given five years and was shuttled from the Atlanta Penitentiary to El Reno, Oklahoma, to the Metropolitan Correction Center outside Miami. My final time was spent at the Federal Prison Camp at Eglin Air Force Base. I served two years before being paroled." While in prison Sonny felt a peace that supported him one day at a time.

While he was on parole, Sonny drove a truck, cooked in a restaurant, and went back to school. After ten months he was given a provisional license. Today he enjoys working in an allied health field. He is also grateful and happy that his marriage to Amy survived their addictions and misadventures.

"The spiritual awakening I have had came from working the AA steps. My sponsor, who is an agnostic, made clear the importance of cultivating an open mind and resigning from my 'debating' society where my ego has to prove it is right. He also encouraged me to ask God each morning, however I might understand God, to help me stay away from drinking that day, and to thank him at night that I had.

"He suggested that I suspend my disbelief in God and 'fake it till I make it,' that I be humble enough to acknowledge my powerlessness over alcohol. I came to believe that the miracle of not drinking could happen for me."

The eleventh step became a guide. "I needed to cultivate a conscious contact with God through prayer and meditation, asking only for the knowledge of God's will for me and the power to carry it out. The best way for me was through meditation, so I developed an interest in Zen and Buddhism. Through meditation I experienced profound silence and peace and gradually came to understand what I was searching for. I began to see that my life was a process, even from the very beginning, when I was filled with deep discomfort, uneasiness, dissatisfaction, and the desire to be someone else. My life of over half a century was characterized by efforts to escape the unpleasant. I craved only pleasure, and became self-centered and insensitive. Now I acknowledged that I needed an interior transformation."

To nourish this transformation, Sonny has made many meditation retreats at various centers. "Now I see maturity as the willingness to accept things as they are, which is the opposite of escapism. Maturity can't happen if I continue to blame my past circumstances. In the stillness I am learning about fundamental goodness, kindness, and gentleness and am more willing to face reality as it is in this present moment. I have come to believe in the majesty of the unnameable and in the mystery and power of grace. Today there is peace and gratitude in my heart."

I learned both what is secret and what is manifest,
for wisdom, the fashioner of all things, taught me.
There is in her a spirit that is intelligent, holy,
unique, manifold, subtle,
mobile, clear, unpolluted,
distinct, invulnerable, loving the good, keen,
irresistible, beneficent, humane,
steadfast, sure, free from anxiety,
all-powerful, overseeing all,
and penetrating through all spirits. . . .
For [wisdom] is a breath of the power of God.
(Wisdom 7:21–25)

TIME FOR DYING

There is a time for dying, just as there is a time for being born. We move from one form of life into another form. The child in the womb is totally unconscious of the meaning of birth; we wait before death's doors unknowing. We seldom have forewarning. Death has always had a fearsome quality because we are unsure about its meaning.

With the eyes of faith, we can be sure that we have come from the Creator and we will return to the embracing arms of Love. Sir Walter Scott asked the question, "Is death the last sleep?" and answered it himself, "No, it is the final awakening." Jesus assures us that the awakening will be glory.

"I am terminal; I am alive though." That was Betsy's message as she told her story to a church group. "I'm terminally ill, but I don't feel like a dying person, and I want to be around people who are alive. There is still something special I have to do each day."

Betsy stood on the stage, looking at her audience. "We're all going to die. Maybe you're fighting something yourself and you need healing. We are all terminal; we are all hurting; we all need healing." Betsy would know.

When Betsy was twenty-nine, she had a radical mastectomy, and her ovaries were removed to prevent the spread of the cancer. The prognosis was good: no radiation or chemotherapy. The doctors told her that she had at least five years to live.

Betsy went for an annual evaluation. After seven years an X-ray revealed that cancer filled the pleural cavity of her right lung. "This was the first time I was really facing the ugliness of the disease. Before I had been on top of it; now it was on top of me."

The doctors removed the fluid from Betsy's lungs, and she began chemo. The therapy weakened her, destroyed her white blood cells. She developed a bladder infection, sore throat, and headaches. Her eyes were also affected, so she had difficulty reading and even playing games. "I came to look like Telly Savalas and Yul Brynner all in one. I began to understand why, in medieval times, the cutting of one's hair was a punishment." What helped through this crisis was her belief that God and her family loved her. And she asked friends for prayers.

A year and a half after the chemo, Betsy suddenly developed a temperature of 104 degrees and was hospitalized. Four days before her hospitalization, her brother, Larry, had been in a car accident and was lying in a coma in another hospital. "When I was sick, my brother had always been there for me. But now I was in protective isolation and could not reach out to him. My white blood cells were only at the 800 count instead of the normal 8,000. When visitors came, they wore gowns and masks. I celebrated my birthday in isolation, and someone gave me a cupcake in a plastic bubble. I felt as if I were in the prenatal stage in the womb."

While lying in bed, Betsy thought constantly of Larry. Just a month earlier, she had told him she was happy he lived close to their mother and could take care of her. Casually he had replied, "But we really don't know, do we? You just might be here much longer than I. It's hard to tell." She had laughingly said, "It doesn't seem probable." He smiled as he replied, "Okay, just remember."

Larry died while Betsy was still in the hospital. One night as she was struggling with self-pity, she suddenly felt at peace. "I sensed Larry was in the room with me, and his presence continued, even after I left the hospital."

Betsy returned home shaky and weak, and soon another evaluation showed the cancer had spread from the lower spine to the lumbar area. This time she needed cobalt treatments. Even so, the cancer gradually spread to her hip. "I had trouble thinking. It seemed I had sludge between my ears. I knew I was dying, and I turned to prayer to prepare myself." Betsy set aside time daily for formal prayer and quiet time.

She found two Scripture selections especially helpful. One was Isaiah 43:1–2:

Do not fear, for I have redeemed you;
I have called you by name, you are mine.
When you pass through the waters, I will be with you;
and through the rivers, they shall not overwhelm you;
when you walk through fire you shall not be burned,
and the flame shall not consume you.

The other was Jeremiah 29:11–14:

I know the plans I have for you, says the LORD, plans for your welfare and not for harm, to give you a future with hope. Then when you call upon me and come and pray to me, I will hear you. When you search for me, you will find me; if you seek me with all your heart, I will let you find me.

Betsy knew she didn't have much time left on earth, so she began making the stole decorated with butterflies that she wanted the priest to wear during her funeral service. She also made the priest's chasuble, but could not complete the butterfly insignia. Her prayer-group partners finished up what she had left undone.

"It was close to the end of the year," said Betsy. "I knew I had very little time left. I pleaded with God to let me spend Christmas with my family." Her wish was granted. She died a few days after Christmas, twelve years after the cancer had begun ravaging her body.

The wake was a celebration. Hundreds of people crowded the funeral parlor, many of whom shared testimonials about Betsy's impact on their life. Before Betsy's death her friend gave her a book that she had written and that had just been published. The chapter on death fascinated Betsy, and she requested that this story about water bugs be read at the wake:

Down below the surface of a pond lived a colony of water bugs. Once in a while, one of them would scurry up the stem of a water lily to surface above the water, never to return. The water bugs down below wondered why one of them would want to leave the beautiful home in which they lived.

Finally they made a compact. The next one to climb up that lily stalk was to return to tell the others what was above the water. Before long the water bug who had suggested the agreement climbed the stalk and found himself resting on a lily pad.

What surprised him was the form he had taken. He was no longer a water bug but had sprouted four silver wings and a long tail; he had turned into a dragonfly. Instinctively he flew through the air, enjoying the scenes around him. As he swooped around, he chanced to look down into the water and there saw his friends, scurrying around at the bottom of the pond.

It was then he remembered the promise to return. He darted down but could not break through the water. It finally became clear that even if he could reach them, the water bugs would not recognize him in his new form. He sensed that they, too, would need to leave their water home if they were to become dragonflies themselves.

Betsy's prayer group surprised the worshipers. In the church each poinsettia was filled with butterflies. Butterfly mobiles hung from the ceiling and the Christmas trees. Betsy's farewell was full of graciousness and promise.

Do not mourn,
but rejoice in the lighting
of a new star in the heavens.
Do not grieve my memory and weep,
for I love you dearly still.
I do not sleep.
Try to look beyond earth's shadows,
pray to trust our Father's will.

I am a thousand winds that blow;
I am the diamond glints on snow;
I am the sunlight on ripened grain;
I am the gentle tropical rain;
I am the strength of the surging sea;
I am the dew-kissed ginger in the valley.
When you awaken in the morning hush,
I am the swift up-flying rush
of quiet birds' encircling flight;
I am the soft star that shines at night.

Do not stand at my grave and cry.
I am not here,
I did not die.

(Anonymous)

M argret was ill with Legionnaire's disease and pneumonia that were not responding to drugs. Her coughing spells broke seven ribs. After coughing for three days and nights, with sleeping breaks of only minutes, Margret collapsed. The house resident, seeing her blue face, finally gave her oxygen.

"It didn't matter to me at that time. I was no longer there but in a beautiful white room that had a golden enclosure. In it my dad was sitting. I was aware of his presence; even though he had died of malnutrition a few months earlier, now he was strong and robust. We didn't talk but communicated by thought. He had come to get me. I replied I could not go because I had made two promises: one to quit smoking and the other to care for him and Mom. I asked him how I could go before the Creator when I was still smoking and Mom was still alive."

Margret felt her mother would be sad if she were to leave her, and she would be frightened about her own care. In spite of this, her father directed her to go to her mother, who had appeared in the distance, to tell her she was dying. He told Margret, "You'll see that even if your mother will be sad, she will be able to deal with it."

Margret went to her mother and told her she was dying. With a smile her mother replied, "If God wants you now, let's say our farewells. I know I will be strong enough to survive with God's help."

Slowly the vision disappeared and Margret found herself in her room floating in the air, looking down upon her body in bed. The crisis was over; her fever had broken. "Two physicians were arguing about the best treatment, and I heard one of them say, 'I am the attending physician, and I will decide what to do.'" Later, when she was better, she astounded the physicians when she told them what she had seen and heard. It was clear to them that Margret had had a near-death experience.

"I am no longer afraid of death, even when I think of it. I welcome it, for it is such a peaceful transition. What overwhelms me is my awareness that for a time I am here and then I will be there. It is awesome because it is so unknown. I am speechless, for there are no words to describe that transition." During the vision she was in a place where time meant nothing. Margret believes that if she had entered the tunnel leading from the golden enclosure, she would not have returned.

It took Margret five years to quit smoking. "When I think about it, I realize that to have followed my father would have taken me to a better place than here on Earth. But I know it was important I spend time with Mom. Now after her death ten years later, I wonder what there is left for me to do because my promises have been kept."

Fearing death renders us
powerless to live.
To accept it
is to embrace our destiny.
The end is but the opening of another door
leading to indescribable beauty, joy, and peace.

Linda's first job after college was at the YWCA in the San Francisco Bay area. The rebellion of the sixties was in full swing, but Linda had her doubts. She began teaching learning challenged and emotionally challenged students in public elementary and junior high schools. Eventually Linda turned to training teachers and counselors at the postgraduate level. At Berkeley she met Paul, a graduate student at the California Institute of Integral Studies. Both were thirty-five years old when they were married.

While Linda's career was evolving, so was her spirituality. About the upheavals of the sixties, she said: "We needed to make change work, but not in a fiery and vindictive way. This uneasiness led me to a personal search for meaning." So Linda searched in many places. She participated in encounter groups, Gestalt groups, body work, and psychodrama.

Religion was notably not part of her search at this point. As a teen she had been a member of the Congregational church. "It was a nurturing church, but I was turned off by the hypocrisy I thought I saw, and so I left organized religion. I was looking for people of spirit who lived in a broad spiritual context. I found teachers and peers to work with in prayer, meditation, dream work, and color work. The Course of Miracles and the texts of Meister Eckhart, Sri Aurobindo, and particularly the philosophy and meditations of Rudolf Steiner were helpful. I found new ways of understanding the Old and New Testaments."

Their daughter, Kirsten, was four years old when the family left California to move to Minneapolis. Linda and Paul made sure there was a Waldorf school for Kirsten to attend during elementary school. Waldorf is a worldwide association of schools, begun in 1919, whose motto is, "When the intellect travels on wings of goodness, beauty, and truth, it can reach new heights." Linda taught kindergarten there and administered the school for eight years. "I found it to be a context where my spiritual search and my professional work came together during that period."

When Kirsten graduated from eighth grade, the family moved to Paris for a year. They found a Waldorf school there too, and Kirsten learned French and dipped into French literature and poetry.

After they had returned to the States, Kirsten went to a public school and was inspired by an English teacher to begin an idea book in which she could express her experiences through poetry. In the meantime Linda worked to make an abiding dream come to reality: to help abused children and troubled families using play therapy and sand-tray therapy. Paul worked as a social worker in drug counseling and also counseled families who had lost children.

Then bereavement claimed their lives. Paul had an enlarged heart and a hole in a valve caused by rheumatic fever from childhood. He had had valve replacement surgery after the family moved to Minnesota, and was living a normal life with no apparent problems. One August day Paul had trouble breathing while driving home, and asked a stranger to call 911. That night he had a cardiac arrest and lost brain function. For five days he lingered in a coma. Linda, Kirsten, and their friends stood vigil. Believing that he could hear, they sang songs with hands joined around his bed as he passed over.

"This journey of helping someone die was a remarkable one," remembers Linda. "After we knew he could never regain consciousness, we all worked to release him emotionally so he could move on from this body that no longer could serve him. And we feel he helped us, because he died fifteen minutes before we would have had to make decisions about the life-support systems.

"After Paul died, we wanted to take care of his body ourselves, and found a mortuary where that was possible. The morticians helped us wash and dress his body. Then we brought him home to the meditation house he had built in our backyard four years earlier. There he lay in a pine casket, surrounded by candles and flowers.

"Friends from various religious and spiritual faiths came to say their good-byes, and we kept a twenty-four-hour vigil with his soul for three days and nights. All of us felt a powerful sense of peace in this sacred chamber."

After three days the family celebrated a memorial at the house. His parents, siblings, and family shared their thoughts and memories in this intimate setting. The next day a small group went to the crematorium and sang and chanted as Paul passed into the next stage of his journey. That night friends planned his memorial service. It was held after his cremation at a nondenominational church near his home.

"It was a service that honored his life," says Linda. "We all lit candles from a single candle to signify how one life touches another and how we are all connected through our love. It was during these moments, when the veil was lifted between this world and that of the spirit, that we so strongly felt the power of love and light that binds us all and supersedes all other things.

"Kirsten and I were blessed; yet with this blessing came an unquenchable grief for the loss of a loving father and life mate. The wonderful memories were so inextricably linked with the grief, and we suffered because no more memories would be made together. Every day we missed him and his wonderful laugh, his crazy humor, his love of life and adventure, and his loyalty to family and friends."

Kirsten turned sixteen a month after her father's death. She wrote: "My life is a confused heap of memories and dreams. Sometimes I wish I could have remained back there—back then. But I have to move on. I will be happy no matter what happens. My tears of grief will mix with those of joy."

A year after Paul's death, Kirsten wrote a poem entitled "Papa" about her father:

Did I swallow your spirit when my mouth was open and dry from the wails of despair that shook my body?

Did it slip through your soft dying fingers that I held like cool shells in my own hands, not daring to let go, and mix with my blood?

Did it seep into my every pore like your living odor, when I held you in my arms and listened to your fading heartbeat?

Was it in the air I desperately breathed when I sang all our old songs to you until my body tingled and collapsed?

Did it fill me like a dream, like a new love, like a body that is the new me, the you-me who laughs and dances and embraces living?

Are you the stream of joy in my thoughts? the laugh tickling my throat, lightness in my heels?

So I carry you in me, not as the fading memory of a father but rather as a growing, glowing child, until we become one and I can let you go.

"I could see," Linda says, "how Kirsten moved gradually from pain to transformation. It helped me to do likewise." But time for dying did not end with Paul's death.

Kirsten and her friend Nina decided to continue their Waldorf high school education after attending a Waldorf conference whose purpose was to expand upon the spiritual, artistic, and nature curriculum for young adults. They moved to a beautiful area in rural New York where they attended Hawthorne Valley Waldorf School and boarded with a family just down the road.

Linda had come from Minneapolis for a Thanksgiving visit. Linda, Kirsten, and Nina were driving to a Salvation Army store when their car skidded on black ice into the path of a semitrailer truck. Kirsten and Nina were killed instantly.

Linda was hospitalized for seven weeks. She lost her left eye and had severe facial and pelvic trauma. In the midst of this loss, she had a significant experience that gave her hope. "I don't know how one defines angels, but I feel that Kirsten and Paul came to me right before I left the hospital, sat at the edge of my bed, and said, 'We're here.'"

The poems Kirsten left behind became a legacy that Linda treasures. "These are some of the few tangibles I now hold to remember my daughter. The profound path of her inner transformation shared in these poems has also served as my guide for letting her go. As a mother, each day facing this unimaginable loss, I question how I might remain connected to my beloved daughter while leaving her free to journey on. I find answers in the poems Kirsten wrote."

Linda collected sixty-four of them, including Kirsten's drawings, and distributed them as keepsakes to the mourners who came to a memorial service. They have been self-published in a paperback book titled *She Would Draw Flowers*. Since the memorial service, thousands of copies have been given away or sold. Teenagers often count the book as their most precious possession. Teachers acknowledge the poems move even the most passive students. Social workers have used the book in teen halfway houses, hospices, and bereaved-parent groups.

Sharing Kirsten's work has helped Linda climb out of the emotional deserts that had left her battered, but not destroyed. She can hear Kirsten's voice when she reads the poems. "Sometimes in moments of deep grief, like on the first anniversary, when I asked for help from the spiritual world, I heard inside myself Kirsten's voice again, supporting and encouraging me. 'Mom, you don't have to worry about forgetting me. I am always with you, in the face of every smiling child and the light shining on every tree. I will be with you as you make new memories.' Her message to me is 'Stay alive.'"

Linda's search for meaning began decades ago in Berkeley. This search has taken her along roads she would not have chosen. The legacies left her have strengthened her and led her to wisdom. She has become an elder, a sage, and a mentor, already sharing these legacies with countless others. She acknowledges: "We parents birth our children physically, but Kirsten is birthing me spiritually. I recognize that grieving is not simply accepting the inevitable; it is also allowing the birth of something new from the loss."

This is a letter Kirsten wrote to Nina the day before they died:

To Nina, my friend,

Listening to "Two of Us" (Beatles), joy fills me, shimmers through me, knowing that although we've made so many thousands of sunny or cloudy memories together, "the road that stretches out ahead" will be so much longer—so many adventures and loves and laughter and tears and sorrow—just so much life lies before us, the "two of us."

(Imagine) how we will grow strong and beautiful (even more than we are now!) and become grannies together: rosy, apple-cheeked, cloudy-haired grandmothers who will tell stories to the grandbabies about iced-grapefruit chapstick and mousse and about our childhood loves and losses, about the hours and days spent together, the years, the centuries; two girls becoming women. And then we'll cackle at each other with twinkling eyes and laugh till we cry. Then when they all go to sleep or go away, we'll slip on our Converses and go dancing the night away under the moonlight.

But that is many years, many miles away. Our feet will dance over so much earth, our ears hear so much music, our hands touch so many people, our hearts love so much! I'll see you golden and glowing with babies, and me too, perhaps. The world will be a little bit better because of us, even if our names are forgotten after our death.

But death won't stop us. It's only another lake to swim, another slight climb before the next mountain peak. But 'til then, 'til tomorrow, I'll remember to love the snow and you'll begin to love skirts over Sorels and the world and life will hold us like a mother.

Happy life, dear sister,
Kirsten

Death comes unexpectedly—
shock waves,
staggering pain
releasing a beloved spirit
into the light and love.

Tilden Edwards, executive director of Shalem Institute for Spiritual Formation, told this story about his experience with Nettie Dillon.

While the nursing home attendant was taking a blood sample from her at 5:00 a.m., Nettie Dillon told him that the day before had been the happiest day in her life. Her five grown children had gathered from various parts of the country to have a last celebration with her. She was dying of pancreatic cancer. Her decision not to have chemotherapy had left Nettie with a great sense of acceptance of her death to this life.

The attendant challenged her, "What would your deceased husband say about that time being your happiest?" Nettie thought about that for a few days. When he came around to take some blood again, she told him: "Endings are so much better than beginnings: better than my wedding day, holding my first baby in my arms, or anything else, wonderful as they were. There is just so much more wonder and glory ahead of us than we can possibly imagine."

Hearing of this exchange, I was reminded of Teilhard de Chardin's insight that "death is our deepest communion." Here was a woman who understood that from the bottom of her heart; she was on her way to a larger life. She was celebrating the gift of this life and her utterly confident expectation that God was drawing her into the more, not the less.

Nettie loved her family and friends, and prayed for her last days to be filled with energy and a freedom from "careless words" that weren't of the Spirit. At the same time, she had become marvelously carefree about all the things she had been attached to or had worried about.

I commented to Nettie that she seemed to have a lot of trust in God. She responded: "There's too much I in saying that I trust God. It's more than trust. It's a realization that God holds me so tight and that's the way it is." She had what tradition would probably call the surety of a real "faith-knowledge."

Susan, one of her daughters, said Nettie was becoming more and more transparent; any remaining hardness in her personality was melting away. Her personal radiance and exuberance blossomed, which deeply touched the hearts of those people who had the privilege of being with her in her last weeks.

I was one of those privileged people. The last time I saw Nettie, she gave me an ancient, unpublished booklet of hymns written by Amy Carmichael, a courageous missionary who lived among poor children in India early in this century. Nettie turned to the verses of one of the hymns and said, "This is the intercession I prayed again and again while I was raising my five children. The end of it goes like this":

Read the language of our longing;
read the wordless pleadings thronging,
Holy Father, for our children.
And wherever they may abide,
lead them home at eventide.

Nettie was led home on 5 August 1997. In the minutes before her death, her other daughter, Lynne, noticed the flock after flock of geese flying by the window, honking loudly. They seemed to be participating in the communion of her ending, calling her mother ever more urgently. Lynne exclaimed: "Mama, the geese are calling to you. It's all right to go with them. We'll all miss you so much, but it's all right to go." Very soon after that, Nettie took her last breath.

It was a blessing for me to be with this amazing woman briefly, toward the end of her life, and to hear from others about the many ways God's spirit shone through her spirit. She has given me a fresh perspective on endings. I don't think I ever again will value beginnings over endings.

We can't have a new beginning without first having an ending. Endings are part of the mysterious economy of divine creation. God seems to be present in the endings in a special way, not only for ourselves but also for others.

In her last graced days, Nettie was a powerful witness to the wondrous presence of the Spirit within and around us, a witness to the mystery of holy endings that draw us deeper into communion with the Beloved.

To accept death as a part of life,
we keep in mind what will count in eternity
and set aside that which will pass away.
These beginnings and endings are a dry run for that final ending.

Robert N. Test (Used with permission of the Living Bank.)

To Remember Me

The day will come when my body will lie upon a white sheet neatly tucked under four corners of a mattress located in a hospital busily occupied with the living and the dying. At a certain moment, a doctor will determine that my brain has ceased to function and that, for all intents and purposes, my life has stopped. When that happens do not attempt to instill artificial life into my body by the use of a machine. And don't call this my deathbed. Let it be called the Bed of Life, and let my body be taken from it to help others live fuller lives.

Give my sight to the man who has never seen a sunrise, a baby's face, or love in the eyes of a woman.

Give my heart to a person whose own heart has caused nothing but endless days of pain.

Give my blood to the teenager who was pulled from the wreckage of his car, so he might live to see his grandchildren play.

Give my kidneys to one who depends on a machine to exist from week to week.

Take my bones, every muscle, every fiber and nerve in my body, and find a way to make a crippled child walk.

Explore every corner of my brain. Take my cells, if necessary, and let them grow so that someday a speechless boy will shout at the crack of a bat and a deaf girl will hear the sound of rain against her window.

Burn what is left of me and scatter the ashes to the winds to help the flowers grow.

If you must bury something, let it be my faults, my weaknesses, and all prejudices against my fellow man.

Give my sins to the devil.

Give my soul to God.

If by chance you wish to remember me, do it with a kind deed or word to someone who needs you.

If you do all I have asked, I will live forever.